ISBN: 979-8-9923821-4-3
Published by Middle America Communication Solutions
Oacoma, South Dakota
Cover art by John Beheler
Printed in the United States of America
First Edition

Also by Scott Woster

Brave Girl: A Tale on the Wind

The names of some of the people in the book have been changed to protect the guilty (or innocent) and for entertainment purposes.

For Big Z.

Deafening silence, but always with me.

The Ways and Means

Truth is in front of you

~

Heaven is where you stand

By Scott Woster

The Ways and Means

Original Song by Scott Woster

I was sized up / I was looked up and down
I was passed over / I was low to the ground
All had gone down hill with me / I was out of place
My mind had a shadow worn on my face

I spend my time thinking / Asleep on my feet
I see the power of my words on people I meet
I'm a kindly sort of man / I practice the art of peace
But when folks push me and others, I need a release

I think to myself
From the time I greet the morning
(until the middle of the night)
I'll work on true self free from doubt (until I see the light)
Unification / Harmonization
A sage acting without expectation

I tell myself
The past, the present, and the future (all is one)
When morning star awakens
(until you see the setting sun)
Truth is in front of you / Heaven is where you stand
You've got the ways and means in the palm of your hand

I lie awake in my attic / The clock below strikes three
Outside is broad daylight / People up and down the
stairs and about in the street

I hear a sound that moves me / Music from on high
It draws me out of myself / Gives me reason to try

With eyes wide open, I search for reason to rejoice
When the spirit moves me I know I have no choice
On a soggy autumn's day or in spring's crisp clear air
Here I am / Here and now / No more, no less aware

I think to myself
From the time I greet the morning
(until the middle of the night)
I'll work on self, free from doubt (until I see the light)
Unification / Harmonization
A sage acting without expectation

I tell myself
The past, the present, and the future (all is one)
When morning star awakens
(until you see the setting sun)
Truth is in front of you / Heaven is where you stand
You've got the ways and means in the palm of your hand

Breathe in
Breathe out
Light and heat
Heaven and earth
You've got the ways and means

Chapter 1

Purification

I was face down in the hard-packed dry grass that hadn't soaked in a drop of rain in over a month. It was the third week in July, the heart and heat of summer. The sun rose early that morning. Though it was not yet mid-morning, the temperature was already hot enough to make a person want to crawl into the cool shade of a cave or slide beneath the surface of a lake.

There were no lakes, or rivers, or streams within miles of where I crouched, bent at the knees with my shins on the ground, arms outstretched in front of me, cradling the sacred sundance pipe with the stem facing the cottonwood tree. The tree stood in the center of the arbor. We called the tree grandfather. It towered skyward from a seven-foot hole in the earth, and would preside over our ceremony and dance.

Two days prior, on Tree Day, I joined the other dancers and supporters to collect the cottonwood from a dry creek bed 10 miles to the northwest. Actually, it was less of a creek bed, and more of an overflow area for the Little White River. When spring runoff became too heavy, the water overflowed the banks to the creek.

I had never witnessed the Little White River remotely close to spilling. During my time in central South Dakota on the Rosebud reservation, near the tiny town of Soldier Creek, I swam in the river or, more accurately, I splashed in it with my daughter. We submerged ourselves but, when I stood, the river had only ever reached my knees.

Tree Day is the day before dancing begins. Our vehicle caravan left the hilltop above Soldier Creek community from the ceremony grounds, where the dance would take place. We wound down the dirt road, which becomes impassable with rutted mud and gumbo after a soaking summer thunderstorm. It quickly dries and crusts into cement-like ridges of clay that direct the wheels of a truck wherever it wants them to go.

We reached the hardtop road at the bottom of the hill, turned right and drove a quarter of a mile on a poorly maintained BIA road, past the few dilapidated reservation houses in Soldier Creek. Then, we turned left to follow Highway 18, the South Dakota highway that runs east-west and cuts a path through both the Rosebud and Oglala Lakota reservations.

We followed pavement for about a mile, then turned right and northward onto another gravel road, traveling for about five miles until we arrived– thick groves of cottonwood trees lined the ditches on both sides of the road.

I drove second in the procession. During dance preparation, my aging Dodge Ram pickup was necessary for hauling flat-bed trailers loaded with cut pine boughs and oak trunk crutches and streamers. These would be used to build the arbor, which would provide shade for dancers and supporters and would demarcate the boundary for the circle of the dance.

The dance proper begins on Thursday–the day after Tree Day–at sunrise. It lasts four days, culminating with the closing round sometime on Sunday afternoon. The four days before the dance are filled with physical labor under the scorching sun, as preparations are made to the grounds for the ceremony.

My wife LaRayne, also a dancer, and I had arrived at the treeless, shadeless hilltop on the previous Friday evening. She drove our newer truck, whose bed topper would serve as a makeshift camper home for us in the five days leading up to the dance. She would sleep in the back seat and I would sleep in the back end. It made for sweltering, fitful and short nights during some of the longest days of summer.

My older truck was loaded with work tools, shovels, camping supplies, and ropes of varying sizes. Those preparing for the dance bring what they can to pitch in and to help ease the load. Preparation is a communal effort. Someone brings a riding mower, some people bring food, some bring tools, some bring chainsaws, cans of gas and gas/oil mix and bar oil. It is loosely organized. The tools are necessary to complete the work that needs to be done. Somehow, all the right tools end up on the grounds and somehow, improbably, all of the work is completed. It never seems as if the Herculean task can be finished, but it always happens.

On the Friday evening of our arrival, the thermometer registered in the high 90s. We climbed out of our trucks at the sundance grounds and were immediately assaulted by a blast furnace of air and the nauseating realization that it would be some time before we would be exposed to the simple comfort of air conditioning again.

It was around dinner time, and life appeared to stand still around camp. People were gathered in their individual or family camps. Others hung around the center of camp and visited in whatever meager shade was available. Some were making prayer ties or prayer flags for the ceremony. Some fiddled with the tarps and blankets that covered the sweat lodges, making just one more adjustment.

Preparation is a never-ending process. Relentless prairie winds and a fairly predictable thunderstorm or two will wreak constant havoc on the dome-shaped lodges. Sturdy and bendable, the recently harvested willow trees form the ribs for the lodge structure, buried in the ground. They are immovable by strong gusts of wind, but the covers of blankets and canvas tarps are constantly in need of rearranging and tying down.

In the past, buffalo hides would have covered a lodge and provided more weight for resistance against the wind and weather. They are a beautiful, naturally protective cover for the willows and for the people praying inside the structure.

One male dancer was cutting paths in the grass, lazily weaving back and forth on a riding mower. The mower was soon abandoned for the time being, the victim of an empty red plastic jug that lacked the petrol necessary to make it operate. That stretch of prairie grass remained only partially mowed until money could be scraped together for enough gas from the nearest station, 8 miles south of our camp.

Of course, the situation worked itself out the way it was supposed to. Things worked out. It happened. Circumstances generally did. Not always the way they were planned and envisioned, but just the way they were meant to. No one had funds for the few things that required money, but we always managed to scrape up "just enough." Exactly how remains a mystery to me, but it always worked.

The "center" of camp is actually the area west of the circle that makes up the dance arbor. The arbor would form a perfect circle with the grandfather at the center, except for the 20-foot by 40-foot wide rest area the dancers use during ceremony, covered in pine boughs to create shade. To the west, just beyond the rest area are the inípi lodges, or sweat lodges; one for the men and one for the women.

Camp central is further west, beyond the lodges and the fire pit used to heat stones for inípi ceremonies. This fire remains lit for the entire duration of preparation and dancing. During the dance preparation days, this area is the hub of camp. There is always a conversation happening here, usually of a spiritual nature. Stories are told. Instructions are given. Life lessons are taught. Mysticism and magic unfold.

People gather here often during preparation, or purification, days. We loosely plan and learn what needs to be done. Our dance leader, Valentino "Dino" Zephier reminds us there is to be no negativity as soon as you cross the gates on the road leading to the sundance. Those who come are expected to refrain from gossip and maintain positivity. There should be a collective intention to do good "for the people."

Dancers are expected to put their own needs aside in order to help those who may be suffering or having a hard time. They have to act selflessly for those who are sick, elderly, dealing with emotional struggles, grieving, or facing any of the hardships that come with being a human attempting to walk a canku luta, or red road, in this life.

This red road represents positivity. We must try to stay centered on this road as we grow from birth to death. We will fall off of this road many times during our journey but, each time, we right ourselves and try to learn from our mistakes.

Sundance is an opportunity for all of us to come together with "one heart, one mind" to help the people. The name of our particular sundance is Okiciyapi Wiwang Wacipi, or Helps the People sundance. The name is a literal reflection of what we are striving to do when we gather each summer. Dino named the sundance and has been walking this road and living this way of life for over 35 years now.

Away from the dance and other ceremonies that happen throughout the year, Dino heads the finance department for St. Francis Indian School. This K-12

Native American school in St. Francis, South Dakota, is now tribally controlled and affiliated with the Bureau of Indian Education. The school was initially a Christian elementary school of St. Francis Mission meant to serve Native students with English as a second language. It was established in 1886 and had 200 students, all living and learning in one building.

At one time, as many as 500 students boarded at the school, but it is no longer a boarding school. It now serves students who live at home on the Rosebud reservation.

Dino did not grow up in Rosebud. He grew up on the other side of the Missouri River, in Yankton or Ihanktowan Sioux and Nebraska Santee Sioux country. He enlisted in the Navy after high school and learned the skills to serve in accounting and finance offices as day jobs for most of his life.

Dino's brother David Zephier began to sundance in his early 30s. Dino witnessed the profound transformation that being a part of the dance had on his brother, so Dino followed in Dave's footsteps. Two of their sisters, Sharon and Patrice, began to follow this way of life around that time as well, and continue to dance with Okiciyapi to this day.

All of the Zephier siblings, including Dino, danced with and under the guidance of their leader Norbert "Elmer" Running, or Agna Inyanka, the holy man who taught them what they know about the Lakota spiritual walk.

Elmer was born in Spring Creek, South Dakota in 1921 on the Rosebud reservation and was the leader of a sundance until he died at the age of 88. All the lessons I learned about these ways were passed down from Elmer, mostly through Dino, who was his helper for many years. I did not become aware of Elmer until his death in September 2009. At that time, I was in my 15th year of work at St. Joseph's Indian School in Chamberlain, South Dakota – a residential school for Native children grades 1-12 from around the state.

I began work there as a counselor in 1994 at age 25, having absorbed very little knowledge about the Native population, the current state of affairs or their traumatic history in this state and elsewhere. I worked with junior high and high school students, and learned as I went along.

Surprisingly, some of the students knew as little or less than me about their culture. Most were just kids like I was at that age, wanting to immerse themselves in popular culture. They simply wanted to fit in with their peers and have fun. There have been a handful of students throughout the years, though, who had been practicing traditional Native ways to varying degrees with family members before coming to our school.

I met a brand-new student during the 2008-2009 school year who fit that bill, but was also humble about what he knew. Shawn Zephier, in seventh grade at the time, was Dino Zephier's grandson and Dino had guardianship of him. Dino understood the importance of education and didn't feel that Shawn's learning needs were being met at the schools near his home, so he applied for him to attend St. Joe's.

Shawn was accepted and placed on my caseload of students. I didn't understand then just how much this decision would alter the course of my life.

Shawn's mother was Summer Zephier. She was a former student of St. Joe's, attending in the early 90s as a junior high student. She left our school and returned home a year or two before I came to work there. I would not meet her until many years later, through Shawn.

Summer had a reputation as a spitfire while she was at St. Joseph's, and she won't deny that. She acknowledges that she might have caused a little bit of trouble for staff with her attitude and refusal to comply at times, but she also concedes that she enjoyed her time at the school and built strong relationships with some staff and many peers. She remains an ardent supporter of St. Joseph's and encouraged all four of her children to attend. Two of them eventually graduated from high school here. One of them was Shawn.

Summer's mother is Sharon Zephier, a sundancer and sister to Dino. For whatever reason, Shawn was not in the custody of either Summer or Sharon when he came to our school. He was instead in the custody of Dino, who was technically his great uncle.

Summer lived with Dino and not her mother Sharon, but Shawn was under the guardianship of Dino and not his mother. Shawn could never sufficiently explain why that legal relationship existed as such, and I never thought it my business to ask the rest of the family about it. It really didn't matter.

Putting aside the legal situation, it was obvious that Dino and Shawn had a father-son relationship. Shawn called him grandpa, but Dino was, very apparently, the consistent male role model in Shawn's life. Shawn's biological father was always absent and Dino filled that void.

In September of 2009, during what was still my first year of working with Shawn, he left school for a week because his grandpa had died and he needed to attend the wake and funeral. In my first year working with Shawn, I had not yet met grandpa Dino. I hadn't traveled to the reservation to conduct the interviews when Shawn was applying to school and Dino, to that point, had been extremely reclusive. He didn't call me or visit the school.

During the summer of 2009, I traveled to the town of Mission to meet with Dino and transfer paperwork for Shawn for the upcoming school year. Instead of meeting at his home, he had me meet him in the parking lot at the local grocery store. When I arrived, he was not there. Soon a small truck approached. Shawn got out, delivered the paperwork, told me that his grandpa was in a hurry, ran back to the truck, and they left.

I knew that Shawn would be devastated by the death of his grandpa. I hadn't spent much time "counseling" Shawn at that point. Many of the kids at St. Joseph's Indian School receive counseling services, but not all. Shawn was not in formal counseling. He was on check-in status, which meant that I would check in with him from time to time to see how he was doing. Otherwise, I would handle social work responsibilities that might arise for him.

He was always pleasant and was still trying to establish his footing at his new school. After all, he was still the "new guy" in a place where some kids had been together in the school and homes since they were elementary age.

I had him come to my office when he returned from the funeral. I expressed my condolences over losing Dino. He was clearly still shaken by the loss, but was able to explain to me that it wasn't Dino who had died, but rather his grandpa Elmer.

He impressed upon me the magnitude of losing Elmer for himself, Dino, and the rest of the sundance family. Shawn called Elmer his grandpa, which justified my confusion about exactly who had died and whom Shawn was grieving for.

This was the beginning of Shawn's teachings for me.

Shawn told me about Elmer leading the sundance and ceremonies. He shared that Dino had been his helper and was like a son to Elmer. Shawn had been going to ceremonies since he was a baby. He sat in front of Elmer's altar and absorbed the prayers and songs that went with the ceremonies. He was nurtured by the heartbeat of the drum and was often put to sleep by the spirits that came to the ceremonies to bring health and help to the people.

These ways were in Shawn's blood.

Shawn and Dino weren't certain what was to come next. With Elmer's death, his sundance altar, both physically and spiritually, would be gone. No one can simply proclaim that they will be leading a sundance or pulling a new altar out of thin air. To do so would be presumptuous and a spiritual misstep. Those decisions can only be made by the spirits, not by man. Certainly, Dino wanted to continue these ways and this had been the only life that Shawn had known, but the path was uncertain for both of them.

I can't share details, but the spirits did show Dino the path. It included his own altar, which was given to him by the Thunder Being Nation, or Wakinyan Oyate, and the Spider Nation, or Iktomni Oyate. Both of these spirit nations are powerful, capable of bringing health and help to the people.

The spirits and this altar are to be respected in the most sacred way. Dino often said "these ways are not to be played with." He cautioned that refusal to show proper respect for these ways would likely bring understanding from the spirits. One way or another, learning and respect would take place.

With the gift of the altar, Dino was able to carry on Elmer's sundance and ceremony tradition. Shawn would explain all this to me while sitting in a square office in a square building at St. Joe's. Shawn was in awe of both Dino and Elmer. They were his heroes. Don't get me wrong–as a teenage boy, Shawn also worshiped at the altar of Ray Lewis, linebacker for the

Baltimore Ravens, and The Rock, star of the professional wrestling world and the silver screen. But his real, life-changing love was clearly for his traditional culture and his grandfathers.

Over the years and more times than I can count, I have heard Dino say "you have your own minds." He was referring to whomever was in his present company, of course, but he referred to humankind collectively as well. His meaning was clear. We all, including him, learn from and rely on our teachers and experiences. But, when push comes to shove in choosing our paths in life, we ultimately need to rely on ourselves and our individual choices.

I have witnessed as people have let Dino down and disappointed him by taking liberties with their own minds when it comes to the customs and traditions of the sundance. I fear that I have been one of those people.

Shawn used this motto and subscribed to this theory as well. He was one of the most accepting people I have known and was able to dismiss most peoples' poor behavior and mistaken ideas by simply shaking his head, proclaiming the notion that we all have our own minds, and changing the subject to something more agreeable.

Shawn also believed that Dino was able to actually see and possibly read the minds of others. He would tell me that Dino knew my intentions without my ever having expressed them aloud. When Shawn was in high school, he helped me understand the ceremony of haŋbléčheya, or going "on the hill" to cry for a vision.

I was interested in delving deeper into spiritual growth and he told me that his grandpa would put me up on the hill. The idea of me, a white man, taking part in that ceremony felt like appropriation of the Native culture to me, but I was definitely interested in deepening my inner journey and learned as much as I could from Shawn.

I had no idea what I was asking for.

Chapter 2

Sobriety

For a small-town South Dakota kid, only a generation removed from living on the family farm and ranch, I turned into a fairly decent seeker, in my humble estimation. I was raised to appreciate books and music and stories. I dove in headfirst and my imagination was always well-stoked.

I was college educated with an advanced degree and had been exposed to my share of free-thinking ideas. As an adult, I found my way to ideas from the east and was practicing daily yoga, breathing exercises, and meditation practices. I was smitten with exploring all of the exciting places the mind can travel. As a counselor, I help others explore their own thoughts and feelings; I have found all of it fascinating for over 30 years.

In the early 90s, I brought recreational substances onboard for the journey and the purpose of understanding the mind better. I found those limited experiences transformative. They provided a new and different way of understanding and interacting with the natural world around me, as well as dealing with my inner thoughts and feelings. My first experience with LSD in early 1992 became a demarcation point for the rest of my life. I "got" their value. I was on the bus. Not just for LSD, but for whatever life, my mind, and the universe had to offer.

I had a healthy fear of all mind-altering substances for much of my life. My dad has been sober for over 45 years, but was a day-to-day "functioning" alcoholic for the first ten or so years of my life. I don't recall being traumatized by his drinking. I have vague recollections that beer was always a part of our life for a while. Liquor was as well, but, at that age, I didn't have the sophistication to understand the difference. It was all beer to me.

My mom experienced it differently. She was well aware of the disruptions my father's drinking was having on the life of her young family. It was still early in their marriage and my sister and I were young enough that it was a tremendous marital and parental burden on my mother. Dad was drunk daily, sick daily and, I'm assuming, physically and emotionally unavailable to her and to his kids for many days.

Dad was, and still is, a journalist. He was exceptional at his job and was able to function in a fog and remain productive. Until he wasn't.

Fortunately, he recognized that he needed help and was able to attend a 30-day inpatient rehabilitation program in our hometown of Pierre, South Dakota. The aftercare services necessary to maintain his sobriety were also available there.

He needed a little divine shove to get to River Park, and he got it. He drove his truck onto their lawn in a blackout. He left the truck running and the drivers' side door ajar as he staggered into the facility, passing out at the front desk after telling them that he needed help. He woke up the next morning and had pretty strong thoughts about leaving, I'm sure, but instead followed their 12-step program for alcohol recovery and hasn't had a drink since that night.

His treatment stint when I was ten was one of the most meaningful experiences of my life as well. I might not recall what his drinking meant to me, but I know exactly what his sobriety meant to me, both immediately afterwards and for the rest of my life. My dad was fairly reticent to preach teetotaling to others, but my mother made it her life's quest to make sure that her children never followed dad down the same path.

Mom had two brothers who followed my dad's journey to sobriety shortly after he did and it likely saved their lives as well. Mom's father, mother and most of her relatives had social lives that revolved around the use of alcohol and seemingly hadn't given much thought to what the absence of it might mean for the improvement of the relationships in their lives.

My mom considered it daily while my dad drank, and then considered it some more each day after he became sober. My sister was a year older than me and we immediately began to go to Alateen meetings each week. We attended functions put on by River Park to fill our family's time with sober activities that otherwise would have been filled with drinking. We learned the serenity prayer and worked the 12 steps.

I didn't know any other way and my sister and I came to firmly believe that zero tolerance for alcohol was certainly the best, and maybe only, way to live life. I made a solemn vow at ten years old to never use alcohol or, God forbid, any other drugs.

I was clear about that decision with my friends and most of them felt the same way, at least until high school when our peers began returning to another miserable Monday morning in school, following weekends filled with debaucherous drunken experiences. Of course, this sounded far more glorious than the everyday humdrum life of school, sports practices and nights filled with television, homework and top 40 music on the radio.

As the evidence mounted, painting the picture that drunkenness could make a person feel elevated, could lead to exciting experiences, and could make it easier to talk to and make moves on girls, more and more friends joined the ranks of those getting drunk on the weekends. Then they had their own stories to tell back in school on the weekdays. I was fascinated.

By the time I was 16 and in my junior year, all of the kids with whom I spent my time were partying and I was isolated as the last hold-out. It was only a matter of time before I caved to the pressure. Sometime that fall, with no authoritative education about how much to drink, I downed a bottle of blackberry brandy on the way to a school dance on a Friday night.

It was a fairly typical first timer's experience, I think. Before the bottle was empty, I couldn't stand without support. I made it to the dance and I barely recall being helped to sort of ambulate around the perimeter of the dance floor at the Pierre city auditorium as it spun in circles around me. None of the chaperones confronted me.

I was obviously inebriated and barely functioning, but friends were able to help me out of the building before I could either get into trouble or make a bigger fool of myself.

I was taken to a house party. I don't remember any of it. I was deposited at home at whatever curfew my parents had required of me, and was able to talk to my mom when she came into the room I shared with my brother, who would have been just six or seven at the time. Mom asked why I hadn't checked in with them when I came into the house. I don't remember sitting on my lower bunk, hugging a pillow and wondering why she wasn't aware that I was drunk.

I vividly remember waking in the morning with a splitting headache and an intense fluish feeling. I definitely remember seeing the floor and my pillow covered in vomit that I had no recollection of producing. I remember the agony of that entire day and my first hangover and the promise, which I made repeatedly with each hangover for the next eight years, that I would absolutely never drink again.

Sadly, I also remember going to a cross country meet at the golf course on the east end of Pierre that day, where I was regaled with stories from my friends about how great I was the night before and how much fun we all had together. Epic. Legend.

I couldn't see straight the night before due to the brandy I guzzled, and still couldn't see straight due to the brandy I had consumed 20 hours ago, but I was a hero to my friends. I was one of them.

We were all heroes to each other, so we continued to drink until it became unmanageable in our lives. What I only dimly realized was that it was already unmanageable in my life, and I had been a drinker less than a day. I definitely went back to the well, but haven't been back to blackberry brandy. Just typing the words makes me retch.

This pattern repeated itself and I only vaguely recognized it until my junior year in college in Vermillion. Until that time, I was fairly successful at pushing away the guilt that I was feeling from abandoning my values in order to drink, to be comfortable in social situations, and to fit in with my peer group. And, let's face it, to have what I thought was "fun" at the time.

The boredom of adolescence leads to experimentation and boundary testing. It sure felt natural for me during those years.

By the fall of 1989 and my junior year in college, the social anxiety I had been attempting to ward off with alcohol since early high school came back full force. Circumstances were piling up and I realized that, soon, I was going to need to face the world without my crutch or there would be catastrophic consequences for my future. I was not interested in dealing with life as a drunk when I stepped out into adulthood after college graduation in less than two years.

I had convinced myself that drinking was something that "everyone" did in college, which actually wasn't far from the truth from my vantage point. I thought alcohol would magically disappear from my life after graduation and I would become, equally magically, the most socially and emotionally well-balanced person on the planet. That was absolutely not the case.

At that point, the reality also set in that I had not been sober during a socially or physically intimate interaction with a girl in several years. Life for my friends, and seemingly everyone I knew in college, was filled with random hookups, or at least the desire for them. Every co-ed appeared to be on the prowl on the weekends, at bars, at parties, in the middle of the night.

"Hooking up" brought status among peers. The wilder the story and the further you progressed with your partner physically, the better. You earned respect and status from your friends. My hookups were fairly innocent, but there was not much mutual respect between partners. Fleeting, drunk impulses, sure. Guilt the next morning over actions that were not aligned with my values, yes. Willingness to change? Not yet.

The mindset of this way of life was problematic. It was misogynistic. I was raised right. I had good role models. I had good values. They were easily abandoned in late high school and college, though, due to the prevailing peer social culture. As the old saying goes, “when in Rome...” I was in Rome, behaving as a Roman.

I am as far away from that mindset as can be these days, but I see high school and college kids stuck in that mentality still. They likely always have been and always will be. Worse yet, I see adults stuck in that rut. They never escaped.

That fall of my junior year, I met a woman at the bar. She was attractive and fun to talk to. I was smooth with beer and was charged with the interaction. She did not seem to have any interest in a one-night hookup and neither did I, so we agreed that I could call her at her sorority house sometime soon to talk more and maybe have a date.

I was excited, yet terrified, for the next several days. Finally, I decided to screw up my courage and call one night in the middle of the week to see if she wanted to spend some time with me. I was painfully aware that I hadn’t been sober on a “date” with a woman in at least a few years.

I promptly experienced a panic attack and realized that I had to attempt to talk to this woman while not being able to breathe or hear anything over the phone due to the pounding of my heartbeat in my head. I was sure that I was going to make a fool of myself.

This terror was not new for me. I could not stand in front of a class or any other assembled group of people and speak without having a panic attack. I would feel panic even when walking up for communion in church. That's a lot of eyes on a person.

Alcohol helped, but couldn't abate that kind of crippling anxiety forever. And it couldn't help with every social situation. And it couldn't help for the rest of my life.

My only other strategy was to avoid all public speaking. I selected classes in college where I thought I could blend into the crowd. I chose my major to help avoid talking in front of a group. As a high school senior, my aunt who was a college professor told me that a speech class was mandatory in college. The anxiety rose immediately and, I have to admit, I gave serious thought to not going to college.

This was not shyness. This was overwhelming and debilitating anxiety. The more I avoided it, the worse the anxiety became. After several years, I knew it was not going to magically disappear and there were some situations I would have to confront in order to be a functioning adult.

When I made my sober, weeknight phone call to the young woman from the bar, I made sure my roommates were out of the apartment on Cherry Lane. As I hunkered down next to the landline phone we all shared, I knew I needed a victory in my quest to sort out my social anxiety and I needed to do it on my own.

Naturally, I hadn't shared my anxiety with anyone. That would be admitting weakness. As a young man, I had been thoroughly acculturated by that point to know this sort of shortcoming was unacceptable

Pushing on, I was able to dial and shakily ask for Annie when another young woman answered their house phone. I waited, passively engaged with a panic attack until Annie's voice greeted me at the other end of the line.

That was as far as the courage I had drummed up would take me that night. It's possible that I could have made words, but they would have been halted and broken by my breathing, which was not even close to being under control.

I hung up. Annie would never have a clue who was on the other end of the line that night.

I, however, will never forget that night. It was an abject failure. I felt doomed. Love and a relationship would never just fall into my lap. I was going to have to overcome the impossible to even talk to a woman, much less construct a marriage and raise a family with one. I envisioned faltering in job interviews and being unable to speak in front of colleagues. The future was unquestionably bleak for me.

I had actually been in a relationship with a young woman until a year or so before that phone call. I had been in love with her since my senior year in high school and we had been dating since that spring. She was a year behind me in school.

I left for college in the fall and she remained at home to finish high school. We pledged our love to one another and both professed that it would be forever. I still had a glimmer of hope that I would magically mature and we would carry this romantic love into a practical future, presumably after we were both out of college.

We had time to grow. Meanwhile, drinking could help me, and us, get through most situations. She was a drinker, too. Everyone in my sphere was.

We made our long-distance relationship work while I was a freshman in college and during the summer before my sophomore year. We wrote letters back and forth and I was able to share thoughts and emotions that I wouldn't have been able to express face to face with her, unless we were drinking, of course. It was heart-breaking at times. I missed her terribly much of the time and was desperate to spend time with her when I went home or she visited me at school.

Through it all, drinking was our companion. Sometimes it enhanced our love, sometimes it did the opposite. When she left for her first year of college an hour down the interstate from my school, we made the easy (for me) decision to remain faithful to one another and to our relationship.

A month into her first year at college, I visited her and we went to a movie. When I dropped her off at her new dorm at the end of the evening, she timidly asked me again about dating others. She told me that family and friends had suggested that the only way she could know if I was "the one" would be if she dated others to be certain.

I let her know that it seemed like irrational thinking to me and I had no doubts about her. I told her there was nothing that dating another woman was going to validate about my love for her. She agreed, but said that some guy had asked her out and it gave her a "butterflies in the stomach" feeling. We reassured each other that we only needed to be together.

That made sense for a couple of weeks, until she called me at my dorm one evening in October. The guy had asked her out again and she was having some uncertainty about whether or not she should try a date with him. She was crying and said that she thought we should see other people, but didn't want to break up. I reiterated that I had no desire to either see anyone else or to break up.

Then I broke up with her. Not because I wanted to, but because the writing was on the wall that she was not as definite about me as I was about her. I hung up the phone, devastated.

To me, it seemed that the only sensible way to recover from the break-up was to drink, gain validation from friends, and make sure that coeds found me attractive and desirable since my ex obviously didn't. Also, I needed to provoke jealousy so she knew what she lost. This led to hollow drunken hookups and conquests while I waited for her to come to her senses and maybe ask to get back together. Some time. Somehow.

Over the next year, we had many drunk conversations and interactions at parties that were always aimed at getting back together. This involved enough uncertainty to keep the game interesting for her. It was a never-ending roller coaster of hope and heartache.

I believed that I was still in love, but was too proud to show it and not willing to fully admit that things were over.

Thankfully, the situation came to a head about a year after the break-up. It was right around the time I was trying to summon the courage to call the sorority girl who impressed me at the bar and unknowingly tested my ability to function in a normal social capacity in a normal interpersonal relationship.

My friends and I were having the party to end all parties at our apartment complex, Cherry Lane, in Vermillion. We lived on the top floor and had an internal staircase that led to our apartment door. We had a small living room, two small bedrooms, and a small kitchen. It was cramped, but, from late afternoon on, it seemed that the entire campus population was crowded into that tiny apartment.

At one point during the blurry evening, I made a run with my roommate and trusted drinking companion Stanley Scares the Pie to refill a keg at the liquor store. We returned to find a line leading down the stairs and out the door, overflowing into the parking lot.

We bumped past the line of people to lug the keg upstairs, only to be halted at our front door by two tough-looking football players who wanted a cover charge and our IDs. We explained that we lived there and were in fact paying for the alcohol that they were collecting the cover charge for. We knew we had a rager of a party at that point (as if the bicycle and telephone now laying in the lawn after being tossed from our front window hadn't been confirmation enough).

As would typically happen, and as I would typically hope for, my ex made it to the party with her friends in her own inebriated state. After drunkenly playing coy and circling each other at the party, we retreated to a bedroom to have our predictable conversation about whether or not we would get back together.

On this night, we took it as far as we could and decided that we were definitely getting back together – we were in love and we were meant to be forever.

I realized her version of forever when our talk was interrupted by the arrival of her boyfriend from Sioux Falls. I couldn't find her again among the multitudes in our crowded apartment. One of her friends informed me that her boyfriend had appeared in his IROC Z Camaro and whisked her away.

I was crushed. We had just bared our souls in complete trust. Mere moments ago, we pledged the rest of our lives to each other, come what may. It all ended with her leaving with a vacuous born-rich football player from a private college, whom she claimed to not have feelings for.

I couldn't wrap my head around it. It was incomprehensible to me and I was destroyed. I was in a drunken stupor, but was very aware of what had happened and was very aware of the acute emotional pain.

I left the party and went into the alley behind the apartment complex. There, among the trash bins, empty beer bottles and used tires from the service station next door, I drunkenly wept. The relationship was finally over and I realized it completely.

Crying felt awful, so I made my way back inside to my party that was beginning to wane and did what I saw as the only reasonable thing to do in that situation. I filled another cup from the keg, toasted my friends and found a random young woman to hook up with.

I awoke in my roommate's room later Sunday morning hungover, heartbroken, and carrying a guilty conscience. Not only did I know that the one true love of my life was gone, but I knew with certainty that my life had to change course. I needed to face my drinking and my morally questionable (at least to me) behavior head-on and deal with the business of maturing.

It was the most existentially frightened I had ever been in my life. It led to truly terrifying experiences with anxiety and sadness over the next year or two, but also led to something akin to evolution.

I no longer look back on these events with regret or embarrassment. I was a young man trying to find his way. I can now give myself grace with the knowledge that there were mistakes I needed to work through in order to be able to walk the path that was meant only for me.

I have solace that I didn't cause anyone, including myself, irreparable damage in their lives. And, I am genuinely sorry to anyone I may have hurt along the way.

As for the ex-girlfriend, I obviously recovered and moved on. It didn't happen overnight, but, when she (likely unintentionally) ripped the band-aid off of the wounds of our relationship that night, it quickened the pace at which I was able to distance myself from her and my feelings about her.

I understand now that she deserves grace for her feelings and actions. She was likely an uncertain, confused young woman trying to sort out the rest of her life. For what it's worth, I extend to her the same grace and forgiveness I have granted myself.

Once I was able to see this relationship more distantly, and clearly, in the rearview mirror, I was also able to make the decision to focus more on being a student. With my adult life rapidly approaching, self-growth slowly began. My psychology professors at USD told us just how limited a bachelors' degree in psychology was and they strongly encouraged us to go to graduate school.

I wasn't even remotely interested in more school. I had never been a fan. Plus, it was likely that graduate school meant the possibility of having to interact with more people and to have to give presentations. I just desired a quiet life where I could work, not speak in front of people, and have everything else somehow perfectly – magically – fall into place.

Chapter 3

Dreams

For some reason, I arrived at psychology as my chosen major at the end of my sophomore year at SDSU. But I had arrived at Brookings as a freshman in the fall of 1987 as a music merchandising major. My music theory background prior to that was basic and I knew nothing about business. I had never taken or even been offered a music class, but had been in school bands and my own band for a few years.

Music has always been my first love. It has always been the one thing that I can trust will be there and won't let me down.

It has been my passion since my dad began playing the Beatles' Abbey Road and Neil Young's Harvest for me when I was little. He was also a guitar player and singer in a local band, the Sensational Standbys. As a result, I was exposed to old country, some big band music, old 40s standards, and some 50s rock n' roll.

I spent a large chunk of my early childhood posing and prancing on our brick fireplace, which doubled as a stadium concert stage, with a fireplace tool or tennis racket in hand as a guitar while pretending to be a rockstar.

In junior high, MTV stormed the television airwaves and my generation was glued to that channel. We soaked up the latest popular music as it played out over videos with images of people I couldn't relate to and with storylines that didn't resemble my life at all. The music and attitude, though, were what drew me in– all of us, I suppose. It taught us how to dress and act during those awkward formative years. I was hooked.

In late junior high and early high school, heavy metal, especially hair metal, became the rage. Boys my age grew mullets and tried to act like our heroes with their guitars and drums who were partying, primping, and flexing on the Sunset Strip in Los Angeles. In retrospect, I didn't understand why it felt a little like wearing clothes that just didn't fit.

I suppose it's at least partly because I wasn't all that far removed from the Lyman county farm where my dad had grown up. He had instilled in me (or at least attempted), most of the important lessons that he learned as a boy on the farm. He wanted me to be responsible, trustworthy, a hard worker, and to be quietly competent.

My mother had grown up on the opposite side of the river in Brule county, but both of her parents had grown up on farms in the area. They owned a restaurant business and worked in a bank and served on the city and county commissions and the fire department. They all lived close to the earth and did not live flashy or ostentatious lives.

The images my friends and I were seeing on television of musicians with big hair and sex appeal from the big cities had nothing to do with our small town lives in South Dakota. I imagine that's exactly why the images appealed to us so strongly.

As a sophomore in high school, the attraction was enough that a few friends and I formed a band called KRAM for the first annual lip sync contest in the newly-built state-of-the-art theater at my high school.

I sang lead and was at center stage, covered in leather and bandanas and baby oil, brandishing a bass guitar, and posing with my mates to the strains of Night Ranger's "You Can Still Rock In America." The audience lost its collective mind, we received perfect scores and first place and we thought we were on top of the world.

We found it so rewarding that we performed another Night Ranger song, "Don't Tell Me You Love Me," the next year with the same results. We were the rock stars in our school.

Being fake was quite a bit of fun, a good way to gain popularity, and it was completely acceptable in the 1980s. It couldn't all be lip syncing, though. There had to be some substance. But, while I could lip sync flawlessly, I hated chorus and singing; I had been begging my parents to let me quit the school choir since I was a seventh grader.

To my peer group, chorus just wasn't cool and it was a good way to catch shit from friends who didn't see it as masculine enough. I bought into that lie, too, and wanted out. Mom and dad were steadfast, however, and I was stuck in chorus all the way through my junior year of high school.

I was not gifted with a great singing voice and, it can likely be surmised that, due to social anxiety, I didn't want to sing in front of people or even be noticed for anything except being cool. I was blessed to have a dynamic and well-liked chorus teacher in high school who knew how to deal with young men who thought they were too tough to sing and dance. She humored our bravado and helped us find the joy in actually letting our guard down.

Somehow, I competed for and won the last spot in the swing choir in a sing-off. To this day, I have no plausible reason to explain what compelled me to voluntarily choose to do this. Possibly I always wanted the spotlight, like my heroes, but unfortunately was wracked with the fear response when I was in the spotlight.

Whatever the reason, I had to sing and dance a solo in front of my teacher, which was as close to hell as I cared to get, but I survived. My reward was that I now had to sing and dance in front of swelling crowds in the new theater.

I didn't win any awards, but sang quietly enough to avoid embarrassment and danced well enough to not fall flat on my face. My real prize was that I learned the basics of singing melodies and harmonies. When it came time to draw straws for a singer in my adult band and I got the shortest straw, I could make passable singing happen.

Again, facing a crowd to sing alone was a terror in and of itself, but I was partially able to carry a tune and sing harmonies due to that part of my music education.

As for actual proficiency on an instrument, instead of just waving around a guitar that was not even plugged in, I failed when my dad tried to teach me as a boy. He had played in bands since high school and was in the Standbys for all of my childhood years. He played in the church choir and was in a big band later in his career, so I was always around real musical performance. Dad played well enough to be able to teach me rudimentary guitar.

My dad suffered from the same terror of public performance that I had, but had the drive and passion from his musical heroes to somehow overcome the fear and perform.

He didn't have the patience to teach his unmotivated son to play the guitar, though, so he sent me to the music store for lessons with a female guitar player from the church choir. She instructed me in the basics, but I quit early because my acoustic versions of Mary Had a Little Lamb weren't measuring up to the rock n' roll that I had been hearing.

For some reason, I didn't take up a band instrument when some of my friends did in the fifth grade. I presume it was not perceived as cool amongst my friends at that stage in life to play clarinet. Boys my age gained status by shooting well in basketball or by evading tackles in football. In junior high, the band teacher was a friend of my dad's. He played the upright bass in the church choir and the electric bass in The Standbys.

In eighth grade, he approached my dad when he was in need of a low-end for his eighth grade band. He wanted a tuba player. The only "cool" instrument that I would consider playing for that type of band was the drums and, even then, I only wanted to play a trap set, which didn't exist in that musical configuration. For some reason – probably because my parents made me – I agreed to the tuba spot and it changed my life for the better, forever.

My basketball dreams were crushed in the sixth grade when the coach set a traveling team roster that didn't include me. Coaching is important at that age, and when the decision was made to not coach some of us, there wasn't much chance of improvement.

My fun at playing football was just about over as well. I had played with neighborhood kids since I was able and loved throwing, running, passing, and catching the ball. By seventh and eighth grade, though, when I did those same things with the football, someone much bigger than me always had license to hit me as hard as they could. That quickly took all of the fun out of it.

I'm not a naturally physically aggressive person. Never have been. That doesn't help much when you want to beat someone up or drive to the hoop or tackle someone or avoid being tackled. To this day, I've always done my best to avoid a fight and contact in general. I've been wildly successful.

I found success playing tennis, a sport with a net between opponents and absolutely no chance of being tackled or even bumped into. I found that I was better at finesse sports and activities than I was at smashing mouths.

I also discovered that I could play the tuba reasonably well. I wanted to please my teacher and quickly caught up with a band that had been playing their instruments for the past few years. It turned out to be fun and I had several friends with parents who also forced them to participate, so we were able to hang out during band practices.

When my ninth grade year arrived, the band teacher knew I could read bass clef for the tuba, so he asked me to play the bass guitar in his stage band. He knew he could easily teach me the basics. I fell in love with the instrument and with the process of mastering it.

After that, the dominoes began to fall. The high school music teacher came to the junior high because he didn't have a bass player at that level and asked me to play for the high school jazz band. He wasn't concerned that I hadn't even been at it for a half-year. I was game and willing to learn as I went along.

I didn't receive individual instruction on the bass guitar from the high school band teacher because he was too busy helping me advance my tuba skills. I put in the time to learn on my own and picked some of my favorite songs from pop music and MTV. I also found some favorite heavy metal bassists and began to imitate them and to learn their styles.

So, while we were winning lip sync contests, we were also honing our chops to be able to play real music that we loved.

We ended up forming a real band called (what else?) KRAM, which was meant as an anagram for our last names. "Bullet" Bob Krier was a guitar player in the lip sync band, thus the K. He was a Rock God, but couldn't play a lick of guitar or any other instrument, so we picked up a hotshot guitar player named Derek Englund, who was two years younger than us. The K in KRAM began to stand for "the Kidd."

JD "Garden Weasel" Ries was both our lip sync and real drummer and was one of my best friends. His parents were willing to tolerate our clamor and to store our equipment in their basement. He is the R in KRAM. Chris "Pitbull Grrrrrrr" Mikkelsen, likely my first friend in life, was our singer and was the M in the name until he was replaced by Mark "Schoeny" Schoenhard, another lifelong friend who, thankfully, had a name that led off with an M.

The only person in the band that didn't fit the anagram was me, so I simply adopted the stage name Brad Aames, making the A stick. We weren't all that talented, but we had fun and we loved it. The ear and musical taste of the other students in our peer group wasn't incredibly sophisticated, so we were the closest thing we had to rock n' roll heroes in our school.

I would lie awake at night, imagining our band playing on the biggest stages in front of screaming fans. In my fantasy world, I would listen to music and always put myself and my mates in place of the actual musicians. I did that with the Beatles and Elvis when I was still a kid. I certainly don't think I ever expected to become famous and make a living at music, but it sure was fun to imagine it. I still do that to this day.

I played both tuba and bass guitar in high school. In the concert band, in smaller brass and woodwind ensembles, in the jazz band, and to accompany singers and groups from the choir. I wouldn't say that I loved the tuba, but I really liked being good at it.

I did, however, love the bass and rock instruments such as guitar and drums. When it came time to choose a future career, the only thing I wanted to do was own a music store and be around instruments all day.

SDSU had the perfect fit in their music merchandising program. I had to have a performance, or instrumental, major to go along with my classes, so I chose the tuba. I actually went to the university in the spring of my senior year of high school and played a solo for the faculty and came away with a whopping $300 per semester scholarship to be a tuba player in the music merchandising program.

I pictured myself with long hair, in my own store, talking about the ins and outs of electric guitars with customers with deep pockets who were willing to pay for my house and car and lifestyle, which would be lavish (obviously).

Chapter 4

Reality

Far from my visions of grandeur, the music department at SDSU had me going to class with kids my age who were experts at singing in front of others. They had woodshedded on their instruments until they had achieved perfection and devoured music theory. These kids wanted to perform for a living, or teach music to kids for a living.

My classmates were far beyond enthusiastic. The more excited they became across the first semester, the less I enjoyed myself. My friends were getting drunk and going to parties. I, on the other hand, was stuck in the music building, sight-singing The Sound of Music syllables and simultaneously directing an imaginary choir in front of a roomful of other students who lived to do just that.

Not only did I have panic attacks in my introductory speech class, which was mandatory, but now I could also tremble and gasp for breath while singing and directing in front of my musical peers who could actually sing and cared about what we were doing. It was worse than trying out for swing choir in high school.

Furthermore, music classes were supposed to be easy. But I was struggling and finished with a couple of Cs that semester, which isn't what I went to college to do. I was supposed to be a straight A student in an easy major.

The experience was not like anything I had expected. I wanted to hang out with my friends from high school who had gone to college with me and to obsess about my girlfriend, who was still at home, waiting for her chance to join us.

Late in the semester, during another tuba lesson that I was unprepared for, my mentor told me I could be "the second best tuba player on campus" by the time I graduated in four years. I realized then that I had reached my limit in the music department. I had accomplished nothing that would help me run my own music store. I was uncomfortable, even embarrassed, and not interested much of the time I was in the music building.

It was time for a change. I just had no idea what that change would be or how limited the choices would be. I wanted to play by the rules, mostly because I had never realized there was anything other than the rules.

The rules were strict and unforgiving. There was a code to live by and you simply followed the path and tried not to look from side to side and waver. I'm embarrassed by my lack of critical thinking skills as I grew up, but I also realize now that you can't know what you don't know.

My path had always been paved for me. I would attend and graduate from college, get a good job, meet the right woman, and start a family. I would magically have the right house, right amount of kids, picket fence, all that.

College was the next step on that path, but now the certainty of a music merchandising future was gone. I now had to find another major that was "inside the box."

The problem was that the list of majors didn't offer anything that interested me, so I did what my academic advisor told me to do. I took general classes to get them out of the way as I decided on a major.

My second semester of college taught me the same thing as the first. I didn't like the classes and didn't yet have the discipline to study through subjects I didn't like. All I wanted to do was drink with my buddies from home and think about my girlfriend.

I finally chose (possibly by throwing a dart at a list of the university's majors tacked up to the wall in my dorm room) advertising as my new major and future career. I arrived at SDSU for my first sophomore semester prepared to tackle classes in the media department, I quickly discovered, however, that the classes were hard and boring and didn't have anything to do with what I thought they would. For the third semester in a row, I immediately felt alienated.

At the end of that semester, I changed majors again and for the last time. I chose psychology, partly because I found my introduction to psychology class interesting, and partly because I thought a career in helping others sort through their lives might be kind of easy and maybe the classes would be easy, too.

Neither SDSU nor USD were known for their outstanding psychology departments, but I still made the decision to transfer to USD for psychology. I told people that the USD department was better, but the truth is likely that I just wanted to be closer to friends from my hometown with whom I wanted to party.

That's what really brought me to USD and to psychology in fall of 1989 at the age of 20. I was in the process of finalizing a break-up with my ex-girlfriend that took nearly a year, and developing a fairly significant anxiety disorder that booze wasn't going to help for much longer. Balancing all that, I learned from my applied psychology professor that the only way to secure a decent job in the field was to earn an advanced degree.

He told us what was necessary to get into a clinical psychology department for graduate school. He gave the good news that, if you are accepted, tuition is usually covered, as well as a teaching or research assistantship which pays a sizable stipend to cover more college costs.

The bad news, however, was that these clinical programs only accepted a handful of students each year.

The worst news, at least to me, was that students needed at least a 3.5 GPA and solid general scores on the Graduate Record Exam, as well as a solid psychological subtest GRE score to get into a clinical psychology program.

I wasn't even aware then what a GRE was. I didn't know that taking it was a requirement in order to even apply to graduate school. Because of poor performance in music and general classes up to that point, my GPA stood at 3.14, not good enough to even reach the starting line to get into the next level of schooling.

Clinical psychology programs are heavily based on research and publication. They are geared towards producing graduates who can work in the field and conduct research for publication at the same time. I am not, and have never been, interested in conducting or publishing research. Presenting research, of course, was a hard no. But I was definitely interested in having my schooling paid for. I was also interested in providing individual counseling services for clients.

A graduate program in a counseling department would have been a great fit for me, but my psychology professor didn't even share that option. There are usually no tuition waivers for those programs, either, so it's likely good that he didn't offer me the option because I couldn't have afforded it and was allergic to debt.

Either way, half way through my junior year, I figured it was time for me to make a decision about the rest of college and stick to it. I knew that I had used up my free passes to just drop out of programs I didn't like. That fall, I committed myself to working hard and earning the cumulative 3.5 GPA necessary for consideration of acceptance to a clinical psychology program.

Both of my roommates at USD during my junior year were also from Pierre. For about 20 of us hometown guys, our modus operandi in college was to stay in our safe bubble. We knew each other well and trusted one another. We didn't have to take any major social or interpersonal risks when we were together and we liked it that way. And, we all loved to drink alcohol and see what developed. We were competent at getting drunk and goading each other into pushing the envelope.

The difference between me and my roommates was that they both had 4.0 cumulative GPAs. They graduated from high school with perfect GPAs and they maintained that through their first two years of college. They knew how to party, but they also knew how to study. We used the library often and then eventually moved on to study at the law school library because the atmosphere there was more studious. My roommate Tank and I practically had study carrels reserved for us in the basement.

I worked hard and, at the end of my junior year, had two semesters of 4.0 work in my chosen major to show for it. I was enjoying my classes in the psychology department. I had chosen sociology as a minor and liked those classes as well. It made a big difference to study subjects I found engaging taught by professors I found knowledgeable and entertaining, but I still had to apply myself.

It was gratifying to work hard and to have something to show for it. I daresay I was proud of myself. That summer, I returned to my hometown and, with the help of USD, was able to gain credits (and get paid!) working with chronically mentally ill patients at a counseling center.

I wasn't doing much actual counseling that summer, but I was supervising patients while they mowed lawns, completed custodial work, or worked jobs like button-making in a warehouse. I earned enough credits to become a senior after losing some during my transfer between schools and shifting majors. I was able to pad my resume with experience in my field, rather than listing the work I had done in previous summers, such as roadwork with the Department of Transportation or working as a short-order cook.

Most of all, I discovered work that I loved doing with people I enjoyed. It was fulfilling and I could see myself doing it as a career. The path in my life was becoming less obscure. I was also drinking less than I had been and was trying to slowly expose myself to new social situations that I found frightening. These were all good things, and my ex-girlfriend was not around that summer, which helped me stay focused.

Chapter 5

Changes

My senior year at USD was a continuation from the year before, with fewer mistakes and more focus. I switched roommates again and lived in a trailer close to the Dakota Dome, where I could lift weights. I had taken up weightlifting sometime during my first year of college and was becoming more and more serious about it. Exercise helped my mental health tremendously.

One of my roommates was preparing to go to optometry school and was also getting married the summer after graduation. We both had stable plans to further our education.

I found out that it costs quite a bit of money to just apply to graduate schools, so I narrowed my choices to six clinical psychology schools in five different nearby states. My cumulative GPA had improved to a 3.67 and I did well on both the general and psychology subtest GREs, so I felt like I had put myself in a good position to be considered.

In the spring of 1991, my senior year, the admissions letters began to arrive and I tacked them to the back of my bedroom door one-by-one as I received them.

University of Nebraska PhD program. University of Wyoming PhD program. University of Colorado PhD program. University of South Dakota PhD program. All of them sent letters that looked largely the same. "We are sorry to inform you that we were only able to offer a full tuition waiver to eight of the 600 who applied to our program. You were not one of them. Good luck in your future endeavors."

I didn't really expect to get into those schools and probably secretly hoped that I wouldn't. I could say that they denied me – it wasn't just a lack of confidence and sheer terror at the idea of a new social beginning that was holding me back.

Two schools, though, forced me to make a decision that would direct the course of the rest of my life. Both were terminal master's programs, meaning that there was no chance of earning a PhD there. Perfect. I really wanted two more years of school and not five. Well, I actually didn't want any.

One school was NDSU in Fargo and the other was Mankato State University in Mankato, Minnesota, just an hour away from the Twin Cities. Minneapolis and St.

Paul form one of the largest population centers within a 10 state region around South Dakota. I wanted to go there because of its proximity to the city and the potential for entertainment value. However, I also knew that it could be more of a financial drain and a distraction from studying.

NDSU, home of the Bison mascot, was in the middle of nowhere in Fargo, North Dakota and I knew little about the place. NDSU offered me and the five other students in my class full tuition waiver and paid graduate assistantships. Mankato reported that they were experiencing state budget cuts and couldn't guarantee me or the other seven students the same. So, the choice was made for me.

If you had told me that my enlightenment would begin in Fargo, North Dakota, I would have questioned your sanity. Fargo and its neighboring border town, Moorehead, Minnesota, are in the middle of the vast midwestern prairie. They are split by the north-flowing Red River.

I had no idea if I could cut it in graduate school. My plan going in was to take one day at a time and simply keep showing up until I flunked out, my anxiety finally overwhelmed me, or I earned my master's degree.

I greeted Fargo in the fall of 1991 after one of the best summers of my life. I had difficulty finding a summer job after graduating from USD the previous spring, but eventually lucked into a carpentry job on a three-man crew. I worked with two good men who were patient with my mistakes and taught me much about the value of working with your hands and producing something that would last. It felt good to do manual labor in the sun each day.

That summer I was also able to date two very pretty, kind, and intelligent young women. Sober. On real dates. I actually went to a play sober with the first young woman and kissed her afterwards, completely sober. It seems silly to say, but that was a big step for me.

Just before leaving for graduate school, I met the second young lady at the Turkey Days street dance in Fort Pierre. I had just had my wisdom teeth yanked, so I looked like a giant chipmunk. My parents had driven me to Rapid City, three hours away, and the closest town with an oral surgeon.

As they drove me home on the winding highway post-surgery, I was looped out on the good stuff. They told me later that I had been singing the Beatles' Happiness Is a Warm Gun as I climbed around and over the seats. "I need a fix 'cause I'm going down." I, of course, knew nothing about heroin and getting my fix, but it still seemed an appropriate number to belt out in that state of consciousness. I don't remember it, but apparently my subconscious knew what to do and led the way.

So, sporting my chipmunk face, I met her in Ft. Pierre. She didn't drink, so all of our brief time together was sober. We went on picnics, sat by the river, stared at the stars, and listened to music together. She grew up with divorced parents and had lived away from Pierre with her mom for most of her life. She had been exposed to an expanded world of ideas that I had not. She was sensitive to what was around her and seemingly unworried about what people thought of her.

My friends and I had never been that way, so I suspect that I was a little coarse for her. She had faith in me, though, in who I really was and what I could become. She was ahead of my time, but taught me so much about life and relationships and really pushed me along the path ahead of me. We dated during my first semester of graduate school while I was in Fargo and she studied abroad in Paris as part of Notre Dame's exchange program.

With both of us back in Pierre on holiday break that year, I behaved in fairly predictable fashion on New Year's Eve by getting drunk and acting like a fool with my friends. I realized that she wasn't what I was looking for yet, and I think she realized that I wasn't who she thought I was. I don't believe she was prepared for my lack of sensitivity.

However, it was a monumental experience for me to meet someone like her and learn so much from her. I hope she understands that and has forgiven who I was at that time.

It had been a fun, wholesome summer leading up to graduate school. Then, it was time to go. My parents drove a separate car, following me to Fargo that August so they could see the new place and help me transport my belongings. We unloaded and went to a psychology department mixer that night.

I met all of my professors and the other students. It was in the department head's backyard and folks had their spouses and kids at the party. I was terribly nervous and awkward, but faked it reasonably well.

My folks and I spent the night in my new basement apartment, which was the bottom floor of a house occupied by male undergraduates on the main floor and by a single female on the top floor. It was affordable and just a block from campus. I didn't much care where I lived while I was in school. As long as I had a place for my bed and television and a place to prepare simple food for myself, I was easy to please. I had lived in worse as an undergraduate.

The basement of this house had five rooms surrounding a landing at the bottom of the stairs. Four of the rooms were mine; the fifth was a communal washroom with coin operated washers and dryers for the tenants. Not only did each of my four rooms have its own door, but each had its own separate lock and key.

All of the doors led in different directions off of the landing. So, when I was throwing up in the middle of that first night in my new place, in a new town, readying myself to attend my new school, I had to move from my living room into the communal area and key into the bathroom in order to puke.

Even the next morning, I hadn't quite put together that I likely was sick because of the anxiety about the new beginning. I was painfully aware that I was anxious, but I had never in my life thrown up as a result.

My parents pulled away from the curb that day for their journey back to South Dakota and took a picture of me standing on the curb in front of a new place. I smiled wanly for the picture, then waved and cried as they drove down the street and out of view.

Shockingly, at 22 years old, I was, for the first time, absolutely alone and would be for the rest of the semester. I knew no one in Fargo. Not one person. I knew the names of a few of my professors, but they might as well have been aliens at the mixer the night before. I couldn't connect with them. I didn't want to make new friends. I liked my old friends just fine. They just happened to not be here and wouldn't be for some time.

I found a calendar and looked for a weekend when I could travel down to South Dakota for one of the big college party weekends. It was too far away. Being here was a certain disaster. I redoubled my promise to stay until I couldn't anymore, and then I would switch to plan B, which I had yet to develop. In the meantime, I decided to wander over to campus and visit the psychology department and study the lay of the land.

Fargo-Moorehead isn't a metropolis but, for the Dakotas, it is a population giant. It was certainly larger than any place I had ever lived. It's not exactly considered a hot-bed for progressive culture, either. Of course, I didn't care about that. I wasn't concerned about expanding my mind or consciousness. My world was plenty big. I was just trying to survive the experience.

All I wanted was to pass classes, earn a degree without having to speak publicly, and move on with my life, preferably away from Fargo and North Dakota. NDSU is a land-grant college and had a reputation, at least while I was there, as an agricultural university. Kids came from farms and ranches where they had been toiling since they were young. They earned degrees in farming and ranching and then returned and got busy, toiling again on the family farm or ranch.

The clinical psychology department was not world-renowned. It wasn't considered to be a great achievement to gain entrance into the department in Fargo. It was one of the few in the country that didn't have a PhD track. Their master's degree in clinical psychology was, as they say, terminal.

I knew very little about the program. I didn't choose it for the professors, the current research, or the psychological school of thought it was associated with. I chose it because it chose me. Plain and simple. They were willing, sight unseen for both of us, to help me achieve my next goal in life.

What I didn't realize as I walked onto campus that first day was that, as Neil Young wrote of his town in north Ontario, that "all of my changes were there." Much of any personal transformation had to do with being on my own for the first time. I had to experience everything through my own filters for the first time. I wasn't doing it with my gang of friends. I wasn't doing it with my family. Whether the experiences were good, bad, or ugly, I had to go through them myself and draw my own conclusions.

It turned out that I was wrong about our psychology department, sort of. We were definitely small. There were around 10 faculty members and less than 15 graduate students in all. The inherent intimacy forced me to develop relationships with professors and fellow students in ways that I wouldn't have if I had been allowed to continue to blend in with groups of 100 students in lecture halls.

I'm pretty sure I got by in my undergraduate without ever having to have a conversation with a professor. That is also how I was accepted to graduate school. It was all done through answers written on a paper.

I never had a professor who knew me. In our program at NDSU, students and teachers came to know each other well. We had small classes together, worked on research side-by-side, helped each other teach classes and grade papers, attended regular Friday afternoon colloquium together, and –possibly most vitally– attended the post-colloquium parties together. We rotated through professors' homes when we had a guest speaker, or at the bar across the street from campus when we had one of our own presenting research.

I discovered that my professors held the distinction of being the "most published master's level clinical psychology program in the United States." To a young man who had no concept or concern about how many master's level programs even existed for clinical psychology in the United States, this sounded pretty cool. Either way, the school was definitely serious about research, which I couldn't have cared less about.

The program actually had some heavy weights in the field of thought regarding neuropsychology, statistics, behaviorism, and cognitive-behavioral therapy. Not many of them were in practice, but instead were more interested in advancing thought through research and wanted to teach the students how to perform research and to become published as well. I simply wanted to learn how to be a therapist, graduate, and obtain the therapy job I had wanted for the past two years.

Fortunately, I was able to complete some passable research of my own, at least enough to publish a thesis. No one would consider my research groundbreaking, but the faculty were connected enough to help me learn how to be a therapist. They provided many opportunities in the community for working with clients during practicums, and I took full advantage.

I discovered that one learns to be a therapist by simply diving in and being supervised, earning the experience. I worked in groups with both inpatient and outpatient adult men who had significant psychotic disorders, such as schizophrenia and bipolar disorder. Most of them had extreme difficulty functioning in the "real world."

The men in therapy taught me much and I felt a kinship with them. We developed friendships in some cases. In fact, one of the patients was a young man around my age who was a Grateful Dead fan. He'd had a psychotic break a few years prior. I had only listened to the Grateful Dead a little in the last couple of years. I heard their name when I was younger and thought they were some kind of death cult group – I wasn't interested in hearing their music at all.

Chapter 6

The Grateful Dead

When I was a teenager, one way to explore new music was to belong to a tape club. “Bullet” Bob Krier, the non-musician Rock God of KRAM fame, introduced me to this concept when I was in the seventh or eighth grade. For a penny or some other staggeringly low amount, you could become a member of the Columbia House record club. Then, you would receive a dozen or so cassette tapes of your choosing, if you were willing to purchase a half-dozen more at regular cost over the course of the next year.

Bob was the number one fan of the heavy metal group Van Halen. He told me that all I had to do was sign up with Columbia House, get the Van Halen albums, and I would be cool. So I did. I picked some Van Halen, I picked some pop music of the times that I may have heard on the radio, and I picked some other new music that I may have heard referenced by friends.

Some were winners. Some were losers. Most of my friends were buying cassette tapes, either through Columbia House or at a local store. My hometown wasn’t hip enough for a specialty record store when I was growing up. When I was very young, they sold records in a section of the Red Owl grocery store or at Ben Franklin's five and dime store.

My friends and I would go there to loiter and study the album cover art while our moms and dads shopped for household supplies or groceries. It was a thrill. By the time I was in junior high, records had been replaced by cassette tapes. Each record, and later cassette, became a new world for me. I imagine it was that way for my friends too, and really for all kids through the history of recorded music.

At some point during my senior year of college, I acquired The Greatest Hits of the Grateful Dead, which I familiarized myself with before graduate school. Also, my summer-before-grad-school girlfriend made a mixtape for me. She included the Grateful Dead's song Sunshine Daydream, which wasn't on my greatest hits cassette, so I had not heard it before.

I was definitely a neophyte in the Dead world. When I went three hours south to Brookings for Hobo Day in the first fall of graduate school (it was the date circled on my calendar for seeing friends for the first time since arriving in Fargo), I took my Dead tape with me.

I knew there would be a good chance of not staying sober in Brookings at the "largest one-day celebration in the Dakotas" with my friends. I had been drinking on Fridays in Fargo with my professors and fellow students and, on some Fridays, I drank more than on other Fridays. I had expected my drinking to decrease drastically in graduate school, but I found out that alcohol is for everybody of all ages, and so is drunkenness and bad decisions.

So far, I hadn't been making many bad decisions. Truth be told, my new peer group of professors and classmates usually made much better decisions while drunk than the decisions I had been making with my lifelong friends for the last six or so years. Here I was, back in Brookings, though. And, when in Rome...

I stayed at my friend Redfeather's place by the railroad tracks south of downtown in Brookings that weekend. My band buddy Schoeny came up from his last year of school in Vermillion for the weekend. Some of the old crew had moved on to jobs or to their own versions of graduate school. Redfeather lived with some new people I didn't know as well.

I wasn't interested in partying as much as I was in listening to music and hanging out. I knew that Redfeather and Schoeny had both taken more interest in smoking pot and had at least one psychedelic experience with mushrooms or LSD in the past year. They'd had a lot of laughs.

I hadn't tried psychedelics and was not interested. Anything that might pour fuel on my anxiety was something I sought to avoid. That's how I viewed psychedelics, as a flame for my state of mind, which would ignite the anxiety to a raging psychotic inferno and cause life-long burn scars on my psyche.

I had, however, used marijuana handful of times. As the reader might guess, my Alateen classes after my dad dried up when I was 10 not only encouraged me to abstain from alcohol, but from other drugs as well. In my Alateen meetings, as well as in health class at school, there was never any distinction made between different drugs. They were all equally bad.

Marijuana was a "gateway drug." If you "did" marijuana, you would immediately be "doing" all of the drugs. I didn't know what "did" meant, either – smoke, eat, shoot up, snort. All forms of ingestion were the same and all the drugs were the same. I was told uniformly by all adults to not do them. It's not terrible advice. You can have one helluva life without ever using any kind of substance.

What I do wish, though, is that someone had guided me through some kind of educated and reasonable discussion about the different substances. I would have liked a more balanced and nuanced discussion. In truth, I'm not entirely sure how ready I would have been for that kind of talk. But I know that I have challenged my own daughter to those types of conversations since she was very young and she has always risen to the challenge of the discussion.

Partly because of this lack of education, my friends and I shortsightedly referred to anyone who smoked anything, be it cigarettes or marijuana, as "druggies." I was approached a few times in my last couple of years of high school with the opportunity to smoke pot. It was a secret between me and one or two other people because we didn't want our friends, and maybe even ourselves, to think we were (gasp!) "druggies."

I think I had a pretty common experience the first couple of times I tried. My friend JD and I tried to get my cat high and took a couple of drags ourselves at my house once. We listened to Iron Butterfly's Inna-gadda-davida and had a couple of tokes.

The cat, Otis, didn't get high, and neither did we. But I experienced guilt about doing something only a "druggie" does and hiding yet another thing that was illegal and immoral from my parents and others. The guilt was likely more a factor of not telling the truth and not living my values than it was about the pot.

I tried marijuana again one night in high school down by the river in Pierre. The plan was to smoke and then walk through a residential area, then up and over the Missouri River bluffs to arrive at the mall and Gator's Pizza, where we would hang out and play video games. This time, the weed worked wonders. It kicked in as we were walking up the bluffs and I was wholly unprepared.

I immediately realized that I might as well be walking on the moon, if I had been able to remember what the moon was. The walk to the mall was close to three miles, but I felt panic that the landscape had become unnavigable and we would never make it out of the wasteland in which we found ourselves. I had difficulty controlling my limbs and maybe even some trouble getting air in and out of my lungs. It was disconcerting to have my autonomic nervous system require my full attention. After all, I'd had full control over them every minute of my life, to this point anyway.

Time was non-existent. We had walked all night, it seemed, and maybe for days. In reality, we arrived at Gator's an hour after we left the riverside. We had been regularly playing the table top Ms. Pacman game there, learning patterns to master the game by eating dots while being chased by blue monsters. That night, the control stick on the game didn't even make sense. The experience of being high gave my friends a good laugh and gave us all a captivating story to tell each other, but it also scared me and I had no plans to do it again.

There were a couple of other times I smoked pot in college, but they were usually after midnight and following a full night of drinking. If the marijuana had any effect, it was indistinguishable from the alcohol. It only served to further dull whatever senses might have been somewhat intact at that point.

The day after I graduated from college in Vermillion, I sat around with Redfeather and Schoeny again, this time in my empty trailer after we had loaded the cars to head back to Pierre for the summer. Redfeather had just returned from Florida on his motorcycle in time for our graduation and had a small supply with him. We lit up in the trailer and again went to some semblance of the moon.

There was nothing enlightening or uplifting about it, nor was I craving it. This was simply like accepting a dare. Are you willing to try pot? Yes, but I didn't know why. I only knew that I had to accept the dare and see how far I could push it. For many, it probably seems like no big deal.

For me, it felt like a monumental risk. As before, I made no further plans to smoke pot. I tried to see how high I could get with friends and that was enough for me.

Then I went to Redfeather's for Hobo Day in the fall of my first year of graduate school. We definitely smoked pot that weekend, and Redfeather and Schoeny took something else that I was unwilling to take. There was a drunken party raging in the house and more like it all over town. We didn't care. We were no longer interested in getting drunk or laid.

We spent the night in Redfeather's room listening to my Grateful Dead cassette on repeat while high. We listened to Neil Young's Greatest Hits. Redfeather played Johnny Cash's One Piece At a Time, about an auto worker in Detroit who smuggled one automobile part each day from the factory in order to build a car on the outside. I was staggered by the audacity to pull off that caper and I rolled on the floor in fits of laughter when the auto worker had to explain the make and model of his car – built from the parts of so many different types and years of automobiles.

We had never heard anything like it. Our jaws dropped when we heard the music in a totally different way. Trust me, the reaction would not have been the same had we been sober.

Nothing would ever be the same. What a remarkable way to pass time.

Chapter 7

The War On Drugs

I didn't take whatever those two took that night. I assume it was some type of psychedelic, maybe mushrooms or LSD. I don't know for certain and I don't know if they remember. I do know that I had two types of fear regarding psychedelic drugs. The first was unreasonable and unhealthy, going back to the scare tactics that all the adults in my life hit me with when I was young.

No one was able to present any kind of sensible facts or knowledge from experience regarding the use of psychedelics. I had one uncle who used them, but he didn't talk about them in any sort of educational manner. He simply, and likely unknowingly, perpetuated the groovy, stoned hippie stereotypes that had been ingrained in me when I was young. Either way, it wasn't his place to educate me.

I don't fault my parents, either. They heard all the same anti-drug messages I heard growing up. I grew up during the 1980s drug war and was told to "just say no." My parents were part of the generation that witnessed, from a distance (at least in their case), psychedelic drugs entering the American consciousness with the introduction of LSD in the early 60s. Then they witnessed the government reaction against what they deemed a dangerous drug and the criminalization of LSD.

They were not told that the government had been studying LSD as a weapon to use against its enemies and that scientists were attempting to discover the benefits, which have now been revealed to be plentiful. Certainly, consciousness expansion and a form of enlightenment have been evident to users and proponents since recreational use began in the late 50s and early 60s.

What current research is proving, though, is what researchers were trying to prove back when they were shut down by the government. They are demonstrating the significant positive potential mental health properties of psychedelics. In the right doses, they can help the successful treatment of depression and anxiety, cessation of smoking, curbing addiction to alcohol and other harmful drugs, among other benefits.

My parents were lied to, and so was I. Worse, I swallowed the lies, hook, line, and sinker. I was 22 and hadn't yet developed a solid set of critical thinking skills. That was all about to change.

This leads me to my second type of fear regarding psychedelics. If the first was an unhealthy, unreasonable fear due to lack of education and outright lies, the second was a healthy fear that came innately from within myself.

I had, by this point in life, struggled enough with some anxiety and depression, and maybe alcoholism. I already knew these were not feelings and behaviors I wanted to sustain throughout my life. They were too heavy for me to bear.

They are too heavy for most people. I understand why suicide rates are so high and why someone might choose to take their own life. If the pain is too great and there doesn't appear to be any other option, suicide can seem the only reasonable act to stop the pain. I have lost several close friends to suicide. I had stared down my own very minor suicidal urges during my junior year of college and it was an awful sight to see.

If there was even the slightest chance that LSD would bring about or intensify existing anxiety or depression, there was not a chance I was going to try it, or any other psychedelic drug.

What I did, though, was pay close attention. I did my research. I asked questions of my friends who had used them before. I read books regarding the experience. If my curiosity was going to get the best of me and if I was going to try it (partly because it looked fun and exciting, and partly because it had been turned into a version of the forbidden fruit, which meant that I definitely had to try it), I wanted to understand all I could.

I was also getting deeper into the Grateful Dead world and knew that psychedelics were a major part of the zeitgeist that was the psychedelic explosion in the early 60s. Members of the Dead and their extended family were at ground zero in the Palo Alto area when testing and experimentation were happening. They were in the right place at the right time.

I didn't know much about it all yet, but knew I needed to know more. I was beginning to realize that psychedelics could be a part of my life's unfolding journey.

Chapter 8

The Trip

In January of 1992, I was almost 23 years old. I was beginning my second semester of graduate school. On a bitterly cold Friday night, Redfeather and Schoeny came up the interstate from South Dakota with some tabs of LSD and a promise of adventure. I had decided we would take acid in my basement apartment, which would be safe from exposure to any other people.

We would be in a controlled environment and I would be with two people who had some experience navigating the great beyond that the drug offered. And, they wanted to once again travel to that magical place. Another old Pierre friend of ours named Donny Dirkensaw came that weekend from Minneapolis. I don't think he had any rational concept of what he was getting into, but he was game to do whatever we were doing.

Taking psychedelics shouldn't be approached with the same state of mind and in the same manner as consuming alcohol, which is what he was used to. Alcohol is used for partying, psychedelics for mind expansion. Donny ended up having a tough go of it that night. I don't think he was prepared for the experience. Again, I don't think anyone should take psychedelics without doing considerable homework ahead of time and without some mental preparation.

The gang arrived mid-evening. Around 9:00 p.m., we all placed a square of paper just smaller than a pinky fingernail under our tongues and let it dissolve. I asked more questions of the experienced ones and they helped me understand what to expect. They said the effects would start to come on in 30 to 60 minutes. We then drove to the store to get beer and returned around the 45-minute mark.

At 60 minutes, I decided the acid was no good and that it wasn't going to work. It was disappointing, but I was somewhat relieved as well. We continued to sit with the television on to a random station that no one was really watching.

Suddenly, everything changed dramatically.

There was a hamburger commercial on the screen and it was the most hilarious thing I had ever seen. I could hear my laughter; it was coming from a deeper place in my being than I had ever imagined. It was loud and it was guttural. I noticed quickly that we were all laughing the same way. In the back of my mind, I wondered if they were laughing at me because I was suddenly not in control of anything – my body, my mind, even my consciousness.

When we were drinking, all my group of friends did was laugh at each other. If there was a way to embarrass each other or put each other down, we did it. We loved to laugh, and we loved to laugh at each other's expense.

With acid, though, I quickly realized that they weren't laughing at my expense. We were laughing together, completely. There was nothing funny about the burger commercial, but we were all laughing uproariously at it. And, it may have been the longest commercial in the history of television. It may have been minutes and it may have been days. I hadn't a clue.

The acid was working, but I didn't know it was working. I wasn't able to recognize a separation between myself and anything, much less understand the effects of a tiny square of paper that I had eaten. It is cliché, but I felt one with everything, from the couch to the universe. Also, I didn't understand the concept of cliché at that moment. And, of course, I understood it completely.

I remember fragments of the night. I remember finding my way into the kitchen and sitting on the counter, staring into my toaster that was in toasting mode sans bread. The bright orange coils looked like an entire universe unto themselves. Just like with the commercial, I had no concept of time. I may have stared into the void of the toaster universe for seconds or for millennia. I knew that I absolutely had to share this incredible glimpse into this ethereal magic with my buddies. Sure enough, they were just as blown away as I was.

Redfeather, Schoeny and I were in total sync. We were in group mind, making incredible discoveries all over the small rooms of my basement apartment. Donny was NOT enjoying himself, however. He disappeared and we weren't sure where he was. I only had four rooms and he was not in any of them. Panic ensued.

We eventually located him in my bedroom closet. He had been crying and his shirt was entirely wet. It was a remarkable sight. We did our best to reassure him, but he remained fairly disconnected from us for the rest of the night, which lasted well into Saturday morning.

At some point in the night, the initial intensity of the LSD gave way to bliss and sweetness. Every sound and sight and thought was so comforting, beautiful, and peaceful. I put on some latter-day Grateful Dead and we decided it was time to sleep.

No one came anywhere near slumber, but lying on the floor with the stereo cranked was sublime. There seemed to be no ceiling in the room, no roof on the house, no lid on the sky.

The universe was playing the music.

It had a kind of reverb and chorus and delay that I had never heard. It was the most wide open music I have ever heard.

I wanted music to sound that way from that moment on and made it my life's purpose to search for it.

Eventually, we slept a little. When we woke up, Donny immediately hit the road back to his college. The remaining three of us went down to the historic Fargo Theater, which had just been restored. It was being re-opened for the first time in years and the showing was The Last Waltz, Martin Scorcese's movie about the last gig for The Band. None of us knew much about The Band at the time, but it seemed like a good way to spend another bitterly cold evening in the frozen north.

We smoked a little marijuana before going into the theater and were mesmerized by the performances from the opening strains of Don't Do It.

It was a transformative weekend for all three of us. I had survived, and even thrived, during my first acid trip. I didn't freak out, I didn't end up in a mental institution, and I didn't even experience anxiety.

The pot the next night had enhanced the music and the movie and the entire experience. I didn't plan to run out and do drugs as often as I could, but my life felt rejuvenated and purposeful because of the peaceful way my friends and I chose to pass the time that weekend.

Chapter 9

Mama Fried

My second semester of graduate school was easier than the first. I was getting to know my professors and a few of them became friends. I began to learn from them outside of the classroom as they shared their reading, music, and movie lists. My mind was more open and was benefitting from these relationships. The other graduate students and I became closer as well. We were friends and were depending on each other for support to get through our demanding program.

I began to plan for my thesis, which would require most of my attention for my second year of graduate school. I also made plans to spend the summer away from home for the first time in my life. I was going to stay in Fargo to study and work.

That summer, 1992, turned out to be one glorious experience after another. I had free time on my hands and discovered all the different park systems in the Fargo-Moorehead area, which is lush and green in the summertime. I spent time working on my classes and thesis in the parks and enjoyed quite a bit of time by myself in nature.

I discovered a local community outdoor theater. I frequented a couple of bars in Morehead that had passable live music and found out that Morehead had a thriving university music program with exceptional performers and performances. I had a new roommate in a new apartment in Fargo. He attended school and played football at Concordia College in Morehead. We weren't particularly close, but he helped me get into his gym at the school so I had another place to work out.

I traveled with my childhood friend Willie Clearwater to Canada and camped on lakesides with water so clear that standing on the shore was simply not an option. You had to jump in and explore under the surface what you could so clearly see from above the water. We portaged canoes in the Boundary Waters and I learned how to play some rudimentary guitar, with the help of Bob Dylan and Grateful Dead songbooks with simple tablature for beginners.

I hadn't been using marijuana and never just had it with me, but I did have a small amount along on this trip. It was strange, but even stranger was that I was brazen enough to carry it on only the second border crossing of my life (the first was spring break in South Padre Island during my junior year of college – a regrettable experience full of booze, debauchery, and a brief trip across the southern border for some shoplifting and tequila in the town of Matomoros, Mexico).

I didn't tell Willie I had the weed. The only time I remember getting stoned was one afternoon while he napped. I spent the better part of two hours on a cliffside above a pristine lake trying to make some sense of Dylan's lyrics to Tombstone Blues and Stuck Inside of Mobile with the Memphis Blues Again. "The sky's not yellow, it's chicken..." Really?

That trip to the Boundary Waters was powerful, but the more impactful trip for my self-discovery came when an undergraduate student in the psychology department found out that I liked the Grateful Dead. We had made small talk from time to time between classes and were mostly acquaintances. He was going to see the Grateful Dead in Chicago at Soldier Field with a friend and invited me along. The Steve Miller Band would be opening for them.

My friend's name was McBuddha and he was from Rochester, Minnesota. He was mellow and kind, with an inquisitive mind. He seemed to have more time to explore ideas than your average undergraduate student. He certainly had far more curiosity than I had as an undergrad. He was taller and bigger than me and I found out that he used to play for the university football team. This surprised me because he didn't seem to have the aggressive, sometimes nasty, personality so prevalent and seemingly necessary for the sport.

Later, McBuddha told me that he was accepted to NDSU – then the defending national champion – on a football scholarship as a linebacker. In either his first or second season, though, he ruptured his Achilles' Tendon in a game. He made a cut on the turf, it snapped, and the tendon rolled like a snail up the back of his leg. His career was over.

I had not yet met the friend who was joining him on the concert trip, but he told me that his name was G-man, and that they had become close friends on the football team. I saw G-man later in the workout room at NDSU and noted that he was impossibly small to be a college football player. The next time I saw him, I was in a car in downtown Fargo with the two of them, on my way to Illinois for my first Dead show.

I had heard from a few people that there was nothing like a live Grateful Dead concert – that you had to be there to truly experience the band. As for the Steve Miller Band, I had heard every song they ever did at seemingly every party I attended in college. They were sort of the soundtrack to the college party scene. Their oft-played Greatest Hits tape was actually a turn-off for me because I had heard it so much. But, the idea of seeing them, or anyone else, live at Soldier Field in Chicago, was something I didn't want to miss.

I bought a reserved seating ticket for myself and jumped in with one guy I hadn't met and another I barely knew and we headed off for our grand adventure. We listened to music along the way. I was already very picky about what I would listen to, but deferred to the guys with the car and the plan.

G-man's story slowly came out on the drive. He was a wide receiver on the national championship contending football team, and he was a damn good one. He had been recruited as quarterback after earning the Nebraska offensive player of the year award as a senior in high school at Grand Island.

At NDSU, though, his quarterback career was short-lived. He was sacked in a game and broke his arm at the elbow when he was plowed into the turf by a defensive lineman. During surgery, his arm needed to be re-attached in a slightly twisted fashion and he was no longer able to throw the ball, so became a wide receiver.

Shortly after we left Fargo, I found out that my two friends liked to smoke marijuana. They were very good at it, too. We got incredibly high for most of the trip to Rockford, Illinois where we stayed in a campground an hour or so outside of Chicago. The forest was dense and green from spring rains and we got high and crawled on logs and made trails.

All of this was a magical experience. It was out-of-the-ordinary for me, but I could see how I could maybe get used to it.

All the while, we listened to new music and exchanged ideas. We had deeper discussions than I was used to having with my high school friends – these guys were kind and sensitive. I was used to interacting with my old friends through put-downs and clowning, joking and posing.

Don't get me wrong - my old friends were kind and sensitive and so was I, but there was no way that we were going to show that side of ourselves to each other.

This was different, and I liked it. We talked about psychedelics, which neither of them had tried up to that point. They both wanted to, though, and they both planned to buy some at the show and take it. I talked to them about my only trip so far and thought about whether or not I would do it again.

Nothing could have prepared me for the parking lot at Soldier Field the next day. There were buses, VW vans, and assorted cars and trucks as far as the eye could see. In between each row of cars there were vendors selling their wares. People wearing tie-dye and patchwork corduroy overalls sat on blankets in front of their vehicles selling t-shirts, tapestries, glass-blown pipes, hand-made jewelry, grilled cheese, cold beer, cigarettes, water, soda, musical instruments and more.

If you can think of it, it was likely being sold on the lot that day. Music blared from every other car as people walked shoulder-to-shoulder between the rows of endless vendors. Every once in a while, a passerby whispered the name of an illegal drug that was being sold, so you would hear "acid," "shrooms," "ganja," and "doses" often as we walked.

I felt very naive, but there was an excitement amongst the concert-goers, and certainly among my small group of friends, which encouraged us to throw caution to the wind. We huddled and decided to split up and walk the different rows and see if we could find someone trustworthy to sell us LSD. Then, we would meet up back at the car and take it. Which we did.

One of us, likely not me and likely with his heart in his throat from the thought of getting caught while buying from an undercover cop, came back with six actual paper doses of acid. Two for each of us. We ate our doses and waited. I was the experienced tripper and assured the guys that they would know what was happening in about an hour.

I was somewhat concerned about getting high and then trying to find my seat, which was in an entirely different part of the stadium than the other guys. But that would take care of itself when the time came. I was clearly out of my league with most of the drug-taking clientele there that day. And, it seemed that most there were drug-taking clientele.

After 90 minutes or so, we became convinced that we had bought dud LSD. Nobody was feeling anything, and, trust me, if you have to check in with yourself to find out if you are under the influence, you're not. When you are under the influence, you unquestionably know that you are.

So, we set out together to look for another seller, which, of course, we found. We purchased six more and hung out back at the truck to wait for the effects from the new batch. Again, after 90 minutes, nothing was happening. Now showtime was approaching and we had a little panic set in. We had about an hour-and-a-half before the Steve Miller Band took the stage and I, for one, didn't want to miss a note, and I wanted to be high on acid.

We knew the drill now. We bought six more doses and each took two, making that six doses apiece at this point, two taken orally every 90 minutes until desired effect achieved. During my first trip back in January, I had taken one dose and that seemed like more than enough for a neophyte.

As before, we didn't seem to be getting high and it was too late to buy more, so we decided to cut our losses and began to move through the throngs of people edging towards the stadium.

I was disappointed that the folks selling acid that day were not selling good products and was sad that I was soon to split from my new friends and that I had to enjoy the concert by myself. I still wasn't that keen on attending social events by myself, so I was not looking forward to being away from them.

In front of us was a high, arcing, wide pedestrian bridge over a street. The bridge led up to the gates and the ticket-takers inside the stadium. As we began our ascent on the parking lot side of the bridge, I noticed that I didn't recognize it as a bridge any longer. In fact, the 70,000 plus people trying to get inside the stadium were hardly recognizable as people anymore.

My mind immediately panicked. There was no doubt about being high now, and I was immediately much higher than in January. My mind was telling me that I was six times higher, as if I already didn't have enough to think about.

I somehow managed to wave my ticket at an official, who let me into the stadium so that I could say goodbye to G-man and McBuddha, the only two things in my world that were somewhat familiar anymore.

As they marched away to their side-by-side floor seats in their own fog, I turned towards the concourse on the west side of the stadium and the sea of people swirling in all directions from there. One foot in front of the other, I made it through the concourse, up the stairs, and out into the stadium, which was sunlit on the warm, late June day, a stark contrast to the dark shade of the underbelly of the concourse.

I studied my ticket and maneuvered my way towards my section and to my seat. Terrified of offending anyone by anything I might do, I simply sat down and tried not to lose my mind. I could tell that there was music playing somewhere distantly.

No one seemed to care that I was there, other than to fix my gaze and to smile knowingly to me. That was somewhat comforting, but an insistent voice in my head kept telling me I wasn't where I was supposed to be.

I considered asking someone around me, but I was a stranger in a strange land and was still a fairly shy guy in large crowds of people I did not know. I had social anxiety, and my head was swimming with acid and I didn't want anyone to know that I had desperately lost control.

I finally looked up at the person dancing next to me, offered my ticket and asked “Am I in the right seat?” The dancer quickly glanced at the ticket, grinned ear to ear, and shouted “Oh yeah, man!” and continued dancing in blissful splendor. What a relief! I was in the right seat.

I could hear the music that the dancer grooved to, but couldn’t place the tune. I again looked up, tapped the dancer on the elbow, and asked “Who is the band?” The dancer shouted back, incredulously, as if I should recognize Fly Like an Eagle, which I had heard more than 100 times in my life, “It’s the Steve Miller Band, man!” I looked to the stage in the end zone of the football field and stared in amazement as something so familiar became utterly unrecognizable to me.

Panic slowly, or quickly (they were both the same at this point) set in. I began to worry that I didn’t recognize the world’s most recognizable band, and that I might not be in the right seat and that I might get thrown out of the stadium, or worse... whatever that could possibly be.

I quickly (or slowly) drifted to another section, all the while staring intently at my ticket and checking numbers and letters on the chairs and steps and making calculations about where I was supposed to be. I was stopped on the stairs in the aisle by a thin man with dreadlocks down to his waist, a beard down to his navel, with no shirt or shoes.

He noticed the shirt I was wearing. I had purchased it in the parking lot that afternoon, which may as well have been in a different lifetime.

On the front of my white t-shirt, there was a picture of Jerry Garcia, the singer and lead guitar player for the Grateful Dead. He was seated by a campfire and was playing his acoustic guitar while skeletons danced around him in the nighttime camping scene. There was a caption around it that read "We are the people our parents warned us about."

On the back of the shirt, in large, bold letters were the words "Mama Tried." This was the title of a Merle Haggard song that the Dead had covered often since their early days. The obvious message of the shirt was that our parents had given their best effort to raise us Deadheads in the right way, but here we were, living the Deadhead lifestyle anyway. Despite our parents' admonitions, I'll be damned if life didn't turn out impossibly grand.

The man stopped me on the stairs to look at my shirt because the picture caught his eye. At that point, I couldn't have told you if I was even wearing a shirt, or if I had skin, or if humans had skin, or if we were all even human.

Some kind of primitive social muscle memory must have set in for me, though, because here I was, interacting with him and showing him my shirt. He asked to see the back. I somehow understood and turned around, he read it, and began to laugh in a way that I had only heard once before. It came from deep down within him, a deep, guttural, roaring laugh that sounded like his insides might empty onto the concrete steps of Soldier Field and spill out onto Lake Shore Drive.

The other time I heard this laugh, it had been coming from somewhere deep inside of me. That time was in my apartment the prior January when I took LSD for the first time. This time, though, it came from him. He looked back and forth at me and my shirt with the largest pupils I had ever seen and guffawed loudly, "Mama Tried, and Mama Fried!"

He gave me a hug, thanked me, called me his brother, and laughed his way into the sea of people. I was left standing on the steps in a puddle of myself, fixated partly on the spot where the spectacle of him had just been, and somewhat distracted by the ticket in my hand and the nagging notion that I needed to be in the right seat in order to begin to make sense of the utter chaos around me.

I did find another spot and was again told by the person dancing next to me that I was in the right spot that corresponded with the printing on my ticket. I was told again, and again, and again when I asked who the band was, that the strains of "I'm a joker, I'm a smoker, I'm a midnight toker" were coming from the stage, where the Steve Miller Band was entertaining the 50,000 people around me.

They'd be entertaining me, too, except I didn't recognize what they were doing as music and I couldn't make sense of entertainment at that point.

Something had likely gone very wrong with this psychedelic experiment and who knew what might happen. I reasoned that it was best to sit still in my seat, avoid eye contact, attract very little attention, and ride this wave out the best I could. The initial wave in Fargo had been heavy and scary, but this time I knew that I had pushed it too far.

At some point, the opening band left the stage. I didn't know and didn't care. I was holding on for dear life with everything I had. Thankfully, I wasn't giving off any signs that I was someone that anyone else would want to engage. After an eternity, the Dead took the stage and broke into the opening strains of Bertha, a song I had not heard before. I didn't recognize the song and, still, I didn't even recognize what the band was doing as music. It made no sense to me.

I did know, though, that there was an energy connecting the musicians with a packed house of what was now 75,000 people. Every single one of them were dancing, including me. It was a sea of sound and color, and it was completely connected. I was no longer me. I was the entire crowd, the band, the sky, and the music completely intertwined. This went on for another song that I didn't recognize.

Finally, they played West LA Fadeaway, which I knew well. All of a sudden, everything clicked and the music was music again and I had never heard or experienced anything like it. I've always said that words can't explain an acid trip, so I'm not going to make the effort here or anywhere else to attempt to describe it in words.

I will say, though, that the evening was life-altering for me. Everything I had been doing to grow intellectually and spiritually up to that point had been in slow motion. This was truly an overnight experience.

I saw the way the mind worked in real time, saw the possibilities of what our minds could do when doors are open and we are not defending against experiences, and I saw what the peaceful possibilities of choosing an optional life path could be.

I knew I wanted to throw myself into this as much as possible.

Chapter 10

M.S. in Social Anxiety

This was the summer of 1992. I had been living in Fargo that summer, my first summer away from home in my life. I was studying and working at my internships and had taken the Boundary Waters trip. I had also taken in the Dead show with G-man and McBuddha, who would become my closest friends over the next year of graduate school. They had their own life-altering experiences with great seats – side-by-side – on the ground at Soldier Field with the band that day.

For now, though, I returned to Pierre a changed man for my older sister's wedding in early July. I was a groomsman and cried after I walked up the aisle. It wasn't my usual way of acting in public, but the emotion of the moment got the best of me and I let loose. I didn't know exactly why and I still don't, but I remember standing there – packed church, celebratory day, happy mood--unable to stop sobbing.

Maybe it was the relief of making it all the way up the aisle in a monkey suit with everyone staring at me. I still feared those situations. I had been in a half-dozen weddings over the previous year and had to do that thing where you walk up a church aisle, as slowly as you can, with a woman you don't know, while a congregation stares and presumably judges. All the while, you are dressed in clothes you would never wear any other day. It's downright unnatural. I felt it in my bones and was deathly afraid of it.

But it was custom. That's the way society raised me and was the expectation. Jesus, I thought there was something wrong with me for feeling anxious. But, I know now, I was just a human being shoved into something that felt, to my very core, like an inhumane situation. No wonder people drink, I thought.

I think back to the Dead concert, the acid and the dancing with abandon to real music. That was about being among people who weren't judging and didn't care how I acted, as long as I wasn't mean. I was realizing that all the gut feelings I had when I experienced anxiety were probably right. I should fear unnatural situations like white weddings and blind dates and talking in public.

Avoidance or drunkenness had always seemed to me like the only logical reactions. I hadn't trusted that just being myself was actually an option, but I was finally getting there again for the first time since I was a child. I was unlearning all the rules I had been taught by school, church, government, and society.

I wanted to be myself, to be happy, to experience life on my own terms, and to not hurt anyone else or myself anymore. I was on my way. But first, I had one year left to earn my master's degree in clinical psychology, which would give me good job prospects. It would provide me with steady income and help me get a house and car and then, the right woman to share my life with. And then kids. Obviously.

Well, I guess I was sort of on my way. But I had to unlearn my way out of the system first. The difference at this point was that I was able to see the system more clearly for what it was. I was beginning to understand myself for who I was, and I was becoming more content with that notion.

To that end, the second year of graduate school was far more relaxed than the first. I knew my professors, some better than others. I worked on a research project for my master's thesis that studied the link between thoughts and anxiety. It relied heavily on research from the 70s that dealt with male sexual performance and anxiety. The researchers hooked men up to penile plethysmographs (yes, they measured erections) and the men self-reported their thoughts and anxiety.

I took that research and paired it with social anxiety research, inviting undergraduate students looking to score extra credit in their introductory psychology classes to participate in my study. I monitored their thoughts and measured their perceived anxiety, validating the prediction that they would have more anxiety if their thoughts were negative regarding their ability to perform an act defending their position in public.

I didn't tell anyone, but this was basically my life story. I would have denied it to any of my professors – I was able to act normal around them, whether I was sitting in class without talking or at parties with them when we were drinking. But, if I had to be in front of a group of people and forced to speak, I would have a near breakdown for a day or more ahead of time.

At the end of my second year, I was expected to do just that. My thesis was complete. It wasn't a particularly good piece of research and wasn't going to break any new ground, but my advisor in the department had made sure that I finalized all the tasks and jumped through all of the hoops necessary to finish it. The last move in May of 1993 was to defend my year-long work in front of my committee of five accomplished professors, some from within the department and some from other disciplines.

I dreaded it for 24 hours ahead of time and didn't sleep much the night before. I picked up doughnuts for the committee in the morning as a lame attempt to win them over–maybe they would not make me say anything.

As I feared, however, they ate the doughnuts and made me talk about my thesis and then answer their questions about it.

I wasn't worried about the contents of my research and whether or not it would go down in any academic hall of fame. I was worried about whether I would faint or black out or have a seizure in front of the committee. I wanted it over.

As I predicted, my anxiety warmed to a boil that morning. By the time I walked into the room – donuts and a year of my life in my hands – my heart was a jackhammer. I couldn't catch my breath, I was visibly trembling, and my words were shaky when I spoke.

For a minute, I spoke about my research while the rest of my body tried to unravel. I imagine it was akin to what serious, long-term substance abuse withdrawal symptoms looked like. Right there, in front of the folks who would decide if I would move on to the next phase of my life. I had completed my coursework and my practicums. I had passed the psychology subtest GRE at the 80th percentile, which was a departmental graduation requirement. I had completed my thesis satisfactorily enough for my advisor to recommend it for defense.

All I needed to do now was remain conscious in front of this jury. At that moment, it was extremely touch-and-go.

After a minute, my nervous system did what it normally did. It shut down to the point where I could act semi-normal. I was able to reason again and fake that I was in control, which I hadn't been able to do during my panic attack. I'm guessing that had to be a relief for the board, because it must have been just as uncomfortable for them as it was for me. It must have been like watching a train wreck. It was kind of them to pretend they didn't notice.

In the end, I received their approval, or possibly pity. It didn't matter at that point, however, because it was over. Now, I only needed to make revisions and turn in the final copy for certification; I was about to be done with 19 years of formal schooling and being graded by someone else's standards.

I had just overcome my social anxiety by confronting it head-on. That was the technique I had been learning for the last several years and would be the strategy I would use to combat anxiety as a therapist with my clients for the rest of my working career. All of my problems in life had seemingly been conquered.

But not quite.

There was a red-letter date approaching quickly that I had been staring down for the past two years. I discovered early on in the program that all the graduate students who had finished their theses were required to present at the final Friday colloquium of the year... in front of the entire department. And guests.

I spent every Friday colloquium for two years in terror. Sitting in the audience, imagining myself up front. Each imagining was as unsuccessful as the previous week's.

I figured I would see how my thesis defense went and then I would know if I finally (and magically) had the confidence to get up in front of just about everyone I knew in Fargo to present my half-assed research. Again, It didn't matter what I had to present. If I had been asked to get up and present my name and birthdate, it would have initiated a half-day's worth of panic as I prepared.

It seemed that I simply was physiologically incapable. I didn't know why, but I knew it had grown into a problem and it had become the focus of my life. I could probably live with it, but it was embarrassing. It was debilitating. It was downright scary.

I have no clue how it developed. I was probably somewhat shy as a boy, but I was always game to hang out with people and to mix with friends. I spent my childhood playing with cousins, my sister, and friends. I was able to meet new people without hiding behind my mom's skirt. I was socially active in middle school and high school. I was often on stages, singing and playing in the band and chorus. I did fine in high school speech class.

Sure, I got nervous, but who didn't? Sometimes, I was even the life of the party. I ran for, and won the mayor/vice-mayorship of the high school by speaking to the student body in a packed theater in a trench coat over shorts with Cons and shades to complete the get-up. I was not a shrinking violet. But I always had someone else ask the girls out for me. When it came to making serious speeches, I was less confident. I could joke and be the class clown, but there was something building. And, I had been using alcohol to smooth it all out.

When I became vice-mayor by running on the "more parties" platform my senior year, I was quickly informed that I would have to attend a month's worth of Rotary meetings, a Pierre business community service club.

They met for lunch every week in the basement of Red Owl, which was the town's largest grocery/department store. It sported a cafe on the main floor and a meeting room in the basement. It was owned by Rotarian Al Kundert, who had his restaurant cater the food for the weekly meetings.

I was overwhelmed by the thought. This wasn't fun. I became vice-mayor to gain popularity and to have fun. Speaking to businessmen in my community was incredibly threatening. And, actually, it would have been boring if it hadn't been so intimidating.

The vice-principal of the school instructed me to just be myself and to tell them what was going on at the school. Simple stuff. These guys just want to have their fingers on the pulse of what's happening with the youth. My pulse was racing, though. If these dudes got their finger on it, they were going to get bucked. But I had to do it. I was, after all, the vice-mayor of the school.

So, I went in for the first couple times and read off the day's lunch menu at the school, told them who we were playing in girls' basketball on Thursday night and in football on Friday night, and got the hell off the stage. I would then sit down at a table between two men who didn't know me or what to say to me. I certainly had nothing to say to them, so we would sit and quietly eat our iceberg lettuce and lasagna. As soon as it was over,

I would sprint to my car, roll the windows down and crank some hair metal to shake it off while driving back to the safety of my peers at the high school.

I knew I wasn't connecting, but I knew I wanted to. It would make me, and them, more comfortable. I humbled myself and approached the last person to speak to them the month before. That was our class president, who had actually earned his position by having the best GPA, being the best athlete, having the best smile, best pecs, best ability to hold his breath underwater, best hair and, most importantly, the ability to talk to anyone and to feel comfortable doing so.

He was Mr. Smooth and speaking in public was like the rest of his life–easy for him. Everything was going to line up and go well for him; it always did. His prospects were incredibly good.

He gave me sound advice, which I followed to a tee. He instructed me to loosen them up with a few jokes and break the ice. It worked for him, he said. It would certainly work for me.

His advice was sincere and I believed him. So, I casually strolled into Rotary the next week and confidently told two jokes. They were both riddles. The first one asked them what the difference was between the food we ate there and a steaming plate of vomit. After an appropriate pause, I told them that a starving Ethiopian might just eat the puke.

Famine in Africa and Feed the World were grabbing headlines at the time. Hilarity ensued.

I followed up that witticism by asking what the difference was between a dead skunk in the road and a dead Rotarian in the road. And, well, by God if I didn't stump them. I had to let them know that it was the tire skid marks in front of the dead skunk. Get it? Well, they did, too, and they really slapped their knees at that one.

Once the laughter (finally) died down, I told them that the kids back at school were eating sloppy joe's, canned corn, a bread slice, grapes, and skim milk. I then let them know what the day's homecoming events were and quietly walked to my seat, where I again talked to no one. Utensils resumed clanking on cutlery and there was subdued conversation.

When it was over, I ran to my yellow Camaro, rolled down the windows, cranked some metal, and drove back to the high school. I was relieved that I only had one more session with them the next week.

A day or two later, I was called over the intercom to visit with Mr. Lonbaken, the principal. No one was called to his office. The vice-principal handled most student interactions. This was highly unusual. I assumed I must be receiving commendation for something. Maybe I was going to receive an honor from the Rotarians.

I was wrong. He appeared stern and let me know that he was a Rotarian, which I already knew, because we attended the same meetings together. He also let me know that the superintendent, Mr. Tessier, was a Rotarian. I was aware of that as well. I had noticed him at our club when I was there. He also reminded me that the owner of the restaurant was a Rotarian. Yup. I knew. Sure, we were all fraternity brothers.

Mr. Lonbaken wondered how I thought my jokes were received. I sincerely told him that I thought the guys liked them. They seemed to be laughing with me. He disabused me of that notion and let me know that I had not read the room well. In fact, the guys were actually quite offended by my jokes making fun of the Rotarians and the food served at their meetings.

I am actually proud of this story as an adult. I sound like a rebel and like someone who was trying to shake up the system and piss off some authoritarian figures. At the time, though, I was a scared shitless kid who was trying, unsuccessfully, to connect in yet another artificial situation in an artificial environment. I failed miserably.

To further confound things, I thought I was staying afloat, so I was surprised by the feedback. I was embarrassed and heartbroken at what was happening. I apologized to the principal and he sternly handed out my consequence, which was to return for my last meeting and to offer an apology to the Rotarians.

I left his office with tears in my eyes for two reasons. The first was that I truly thought I was one of The Guys and was blindsided that I had read the room that poorly. The second was that I now had to walk back into that room and share an emotional apology, which would undoubtedly be more brutal for me than reading the lunch menu or telling a clever (or otherwise) joke or two.

I dreaded my last meeting with the Rotarians and somehow choked out a heartfelt apology to a bunch of grown men who I now realized were not my friends. I wasn't a part of their club. I was just another face filling a spot on their meeting agenda. They would have a different one next month.

I don't remember much about the apology and I don't remember any of the men acknowledging my contrition. None of them reached out to a 17-year-old kid to discuss the situation and let me know that I could recover from it, possibly even grow from such a complex social mistake. I imagine I was labeled by some of them. I can agree that I probably even deserved a label.

Now, I can look back and realize I was just a kid trying to sort out life. At the time, I only knew I was an abject failure at public speaking and at trying to survive social situations in an adult world. Adults saw me as an offensive, insensitive jerk. I assumed that I would magically sort it all out when I became an actual adult, but that mattered little early on in my senior year when I was still a damn sight from being mature.

Chapter 11

Origins of Fear

Truth be told, I might not have even been that good at sorting out social complexities with my peer group. Two of the most difficult things – the most important to young people at that age – are determining where you stand with your friends and trying to navigate the romantic road map.

I don't want to overstate my personal problems with either because I was generally well-liked and had a close group of friends. I also did well at dating. Since the sixth grade, I usually had a girl that I was "going out with." My friends always did the heavy lifting to make it happen, though. If I liked someone, they would check with her or her friends to find out if it was mutual. If it was mutual, my friend would ask the girl out for me.

If there was a break-up, the friend would let the girl know that I was breaking up with her. If a girl was breaking up with me, they would generally let me know through their friends as well. There came a time, though, when it became embarrassing to have to use friends for this. There was supposed to be an age when you did the work yourself. I'm pretty sure I never reached that age.

So, although I was always involved in romantic relationships, I always luckily and happily just stumbled into them. It was passive and most of my interactions within the relationships were passive as well. Then booze came along and did the heavy lifting that my friends had always done. Get a nice buzz on, or even full-on shitfaced, and I could talk to anybody about almost anything.

I hadn't planned to drink at all in my life but, after I began when I was well into my 16th year, it just became too easy. It made Friday and Saturday nights feel much more special for the rest of high school, in the summer after high school, and for the first few years of college... Until it didn't make them feel special. After that, it just made them feel unhealthy, shameful, and maladaptive.

Ever since I became aware of "college," I had always planned to attend South Dakota State University. My dad went to school there, as did his sister and two brothers. We would attend Jackrabbit football and basketball games there yearly and my aunt taught in the English department there for most of her career. There wasn't much chance of me going elsewhere. My sister went the year before I did. She went on to teach English there. My younger brother graduated from there and went on to teach in the Psychology department.

During my senior year of high school, my professor aunt told me that speech classes were mandatory for coursework and graduation at SDSU. I immediately felt panic and half-joked that I would now not be attending college. I was also half-serious and had a visceral panic reaction anytime I would think about speaking in a college classroom in front of people I didn't even know.

I considered drinking before my speeches, but I knew that could be interpreted as a sign of becoming an alcoholic, and I certainly didn't want that. I just wanted to drink and have fun for a few years and then live a perfect life as an adult.

Obviously, I attended SDSU for a couple of years and was able to pass that Intro to Speech class the first semester I was there. It was painful, though. I wrote decent speeches and the night before I would stand in front of my dorm room mirror when my roommate was out and perform my timed speech for the imaginary audience. I wouldn't dedicate more than the exact time limit the professor required. I would then be in a state of anticipatory dread until the anxiety peaked as I walked up to give my speech in class.

I remember my knees wobbling under me and my hands shaking badly enough that I had to work to follow the 3 x 5 index cards containing my notes as they bounced in my field of vision. I couldn't catch my breath, so my voice trembled. I felt myself gasping to breathe and speak at the same time.

None of the thirty or so classmates seemed to notice or care that I had even given a speech, but that didn't matter. The only thing that mattered was my internal dialogue about how painful the experience was.

When the speeches were over, there was always sheer relief. Sure, there was some residual physiological residue like mild trembling. The normal kind of bodily feeling one might have after a traumatic experience. But psychologically, all I felt was relief that it was over.

It felt good to have them done, but there was always a slightly haunting feeling deep inside that life was going to be rough if I continued to shit the bed every time I had to talk in front of people. I could mostly ignore that feeling, at least until the next presentation.

Of course, ignoring a phobia only makes it worse, as I was learning in all of my psychology classes, the focus of my two degrees. Even with that knowledge, I would avoid opportunities to speak like the plague. I couldn't quite bring myself to summon the courage I needed to approach my fears and conquer them.

Chapter 12

Escape

This all brings me back to the colloquium presentation I had to make before leaving Fargo with a completed master's degree. It was required by my department and likely a necessary step in my process of self-development, but didn't affect my grade and likely wouldn't keep me from graduating. Plus, there was no make-up date. Bail once, bail for good.

I called the school on the morning of colloquium to let the department secretary know that I was under the weather and wouldn't be able to attend that day. She said she would let the professors know. That was that. I never heard another word about it, but it haunted me for years.

After the call, I jumped into my 1988 GMC Jimmy and drove east on I-94 a couple of hours to see Blues Traveler play at Collegeville, Minnesota. For the past few months, I had been dating a girl from my hometown who attended the all-girls college there. I have no recollection of how the relationship began, but I can only presume I did not instigate it. Not because I didn't like her, she was great. I just couldn't see myself being brave enough at that point to reach out to begin that, or any other, relationship.

I was, however, brave enough to end it on my own a couple of months later when it didn't feel quite right. That was a big step for me. I doubt she was applauding me for my newfound courage, and likely wasn't impressed with the size of the steps I was taking. I didn't like rejecting someone I cared about, but I did like that I did it myself.

Two months before that, though, the two of us had a splendid time dancing under the May sun as Blues Traveler tore through their set in front of a small crowd on St. John's campus.

Meanwhile, my graduate school classmates acted like mature adults and presented their research in front of each other, faculty, and distinguished guests.

I had a nagging feeling that I should have stayed to give my presentation, but I wasn't going to let it bring me down that day. I was in suppression mode. There would be plenty of time for regrets about it later, if my social anxiety didn't magically disappear with the completion of my master's degree, as I hoped it would.

It turned out that it didn't disappear in adulthood. It also turned out that there was going to be plenty of time for it to bring me down.

I discovered that it is even more embarrassing to have an adult career and to have panic attacks about speaking in public. I'm talking about small meetings with your co-workers and other groups where you simply have to say your name, where you're from, and how long you've been at your current job.

I struggled with it for many years. I've been a counselor at St. Joseph's Indian School for 31 years as of this writing. I interviewed for and began the job when I was 25 years old in July 1994. Social anxiety crippled me for a long time. Had I been able to face down my fear that day that I skipped colloquium, I don't think the anxiety would have ended.

It sure would have been embarrassing to have a panic attack in front of everyone I knew in that world, but playing hooky that day still brings me shame.

Chapter 13

On the Bus

A week after skipping the colloquium, I turned in the final copy of my thesis and jumped in my 1988 GMC Jimmy with my buddy G-man, of Chicago Dead concert fame. We headed west to tour as Deadheads and, as he said when I woke him up on the first morning of the trip, to "eat the grass and drink the rain."

This trip was intended as a last hurrah before getting serious about the rest of our lives. I was also interested in scoping out the country to look for cool places where I might live out the rest of my life. So far, I had lived in Pierre, Brookings, and Vermillion, South Dakota, and then Fargo, North Dakota.

It was time for a change. I was destined for a bigger place with much more to offer, including some anonymity. I was ready to break out on my own after finding myself able to survive in North Dakota by myself.

Most importantly, though, it was time to watch the Grateful Dead play live. The concert in Chicago the year before was life-changing for me and I was "on the bus."

During my second year of graduate school, I was soaking up as much of their music as I could find.

Obtaining music was different back then. I bought studio compact discs at Best Buy in Fargo and I was able to gather a few concert cassettes from people I met in Fargo who listened to the Dead –there just wasn't much music available. I had every note and lyric on the tapes and CDs in my possession memorized. Nowadays, I can just go on the internet and find every concert they ever played, but that's not how it worked then.

I had one book on the history of the band, loaned to me by a schizophrenic young adult male client from my earlier practicum, and some studio tapes that I recorded from my professors. I also had a songbook with tablature so I could learn to play a few of the songs I was getting to know. I borrowed my dad's acoustic guitar and learned simple chords to some of the songs during the trip.

I hadn't played in a band since high school, but I still had my bass and amp. On a few occasions during my second year of grad school, I got together with two of my professors who played some guitar. I don't remember much of the music, but I do remember that one of the times we played they got me so stoned I couldn't make much sense of my bass guitar.

I wasn't smoking pot in that second year and I wasn't drinking very much, either. Craft beers were becoming more and more popular and the gargantuan Happy Harry's liquor store carried quite a selection to try. Instead of drinking a 12-pack of Busch Light, it was more likely that I would have a couple Guinness or Samuel Adams or Anchor Steam or Sierra Nevada pale ales. A drunken night had finally become a rarity.

I was keeping an eye on my friend McBuddha from the Chicago Dead show as well. In any given situation, he was as likely to be stoned as he was to be sober. I couldn't tell the difference. He was the first guy I knew who didn't get stoned just to party. He got stoned to read books and enjoy food and to listen to music or to chill with friends.

I was paying attention and it was revelatory for me that a drug could be used for something other than a party. I still wasn't using much of it, but I was understanding and respecting it more and more.

In May of 1993 when G-man and I headed west, we had a small amount of marijuana. We stayed with Garden Weasel, of KRAM percussion fame, and his wife at Pacific University outside of Portland, Oregon, where they were both studying for a career in optometry. We crested the coastal mountain range to get to the beaches and the ocean, then drove south on highway 1 down to San Francisco: ground zero for the Grateful Dead.

It was a given that the Dead and LSD went hand in hand, so we were able to find some for our first show of the tour. We were in the heart of what is now Silicon Valley at Shoreline Amphitheater in Mountain View, California. We had some idea of how to handle that intense LSD high now and we had a wonderful time.

We had good reserved seats and I had no doubt that I was in the right seat this time. Everything in the universe lined up at that show, just as I knew it should. It was a perfect feeling. I was becoming more familiar with the music now. At that show, I bought a book with interviews with the band and read it cover to cover as we drove to the next show. I couldn't get enough.

The next stop was Sacramento. It was general admission seating at an old race track at the Cal-Expo fairgrounds. G-man and I again took LSD before the show and we had our first inkling of what could possibly go wrong with the drug. It didn't provide the same comfort as it had at the first show or the two other times I had taken it.

We watched a Frenchman struggle with a bad trip in the middle of the crowd that day and we were both affected. He "freaked out," spoke nothing but French, and it confirmed our worst fears about what psychedelics could do when it went badly.

The show wasn't our favorite and G-man made the decision the next day that he was going to take a bus back to Fargo to be with his girlfriend, whom he was missing.

I was in my element, though, and there was no possibility that I was going home. I drove down to Santa Barbara to spend the evening with one of my NDSU professors who had just taken a job at UCSB. Santa Barbara was beautiful. He took me out for dinner with a friend and we talked about books and ideas. We then trespassed onto a private beach and watched the sun drop on the far side of the Pacific Ocean.

All the while, we smoked his marijuana, which was exceptional, and exceptionally strong. I was beginning to enjoy the chill aspect of smoking and it seemed like, on this trip at least, everyone was doing it.

I drove across the desert the next day with my new Dead book opened on the steering wheel and my Dead cassettes on the tape deck. The glossary of the book contained a listing of all of the cover songs played by the Dead and went into detail regarding the origins of each song. It opened a world of new musical avenues for me. Performers and genres that I would never have been exposed to were now in my grasp thanks to my connection to the Dead.

Deadheads are easy to talk to and I had many conversations in the parking lots, waiting in lines, sitting in my seat at shows, and at stops along the road with fellow travelers. I learned so much that I wouldn't have otherwise been exposed to, had I not ventured out and traveled with the Dead that summer.

For better and/or worse, I was taking some risks, too. I had a small amount of weed and a small amount of acid on me most of the trip, either of which could have earned me significant jail time due to the ridiculous mandatory minimum sentencing laws. I didn't have to agree with the laws, but I certainly would have to respect them if I got busted.

I went to Houston to stay for a few days with Schoeny, who was living and working there. We spent several days together, taking acid, smoking pot, and listening to the Dead. It was a grand experience. Houston is a god-awful place, all concrete and steel and people. It's even worse during the summer months. I arrived at the end of May or beginning of June. It was scorchingly hot.

Schoeny had graduated from the University of South Dakota business school recently and had jumped in the queue to apply for a sales position with Warren Moon's

Mattress Firm. They sent representatives, or head-hunters, to South Dakota and the nationally recognized USD business school to find graduates with strong Midwestern work ethic to come down south and be a part of their franchise.

Schoeny was never keen on college, or school at any level, and likely was never too excited about the business school. He went to college to be with friends and ended up with a business degree. But he found a job in Houston with the Mattress Firm because of it.

Schoeny had a friend at the business school who was actually from Pierre and graduated with him from high school. This friend didn't hang around with our crowd, but ended up being Schoeny's roommate for his last year at USD after the rest of us had graduated and moved on because we were a year older. This friend and Schoeny used drugs more heavily during their last year at USD. This friend also moved down to the Houston area and was also working for the Mattress Firm.

Schoeny's life at that time involved a button-up shirt, tie and slacks. He peddled mattresses out the front door while peddling various drugs out the back door. Of course, he was using some of those drugs himself, both on the job and in his spare time.

He had discovered the Dead, mostly through me, but had not seen them in concert and wasn't as into them as I was yet. That was all to change after we spent several days staring at candles in his bedroom while listening to concert tapes and talking about them, when words were necessary.

We had a miniature acid test renaissance in Houston, which took some of the oppression off of the hundred degree weather and the steel buildings and concrete parkways. Acid couldn't take the coldness out of the Houston Astrodome, though. We had tickets for a game there, and the most interesting thing from a nine-inning game was a bird that caught our attention, flying haphazard aps in front of us all the way through the event.

I deserted Schoeny in that desolate place with a promise to mail him more acid when I could find some later in the trip. I then drove alone across swamp country in Louisiana and through the panhandle of Florida. I have to say there was nothing remarkable about the area. But I had seen it and now knew there wasn't anything that would entice me to return there.

I turned left when I hit the Atlantic ocean and trekked northward. Filing north on Interstate 95, all I saw were bumpers and license plates and trees on either side of the road. That is the interstate view and what I remember from driving north.

I carried a small cooler in the back of my '88 Jimmy and I stocked it with bologna and cheese and bread and maybe some apples from time to time. I ate when I was hungry and pulled over to sleep in rest areas in the back of the vehicle when I needed to.

I had a box of well-worn paperbacks my dad had given me prior to the trip. They were paperbacks, hand-picked from his collection. There were novels by Jean Paul Sartre, John Updike, John Irving, Saul Bellow, and Thomas Pynchon. They kept me occupied in the back of the Jimmy and I couldn't have been happier during my downtime.

I had never seen that many cars or people. There were no open spaces, no prairies. There was no view. You can't see the ocean from Interstate 95, and I didn't have time for detours. I was bound for New York City for the next Dead show.

The only stop I made along the route was in Washington DC. I thought it might be kind of fun to see a few of the monuments and to be able to say that I had been there. Little did I know that the city was designed in concentric circles for defense purposes and that I would find myself driving in circles, occasionally passing the

Lincoln Memorial close enough to see it, but not close enough to find a way to get to it or a place to park.

Ultimately, I was able to pull in somewhere, find a parking spot, and walk the length of the Capital Mall. I vowed that I would come back when I knew more about where to go and had more time to experience a bigger sample of Washington DC. It piqued my interest in history.

The east coast was new to me, having never been farther than Detroit. Even then, I had flown to Detroit in high school, so I didn't see much of the countryside. South Dakota had 700,000 people in the entire state. It seemed that there were at least that many squeezed into every square mile from Washington DC all the way up to New York City. It was overwhelming. So was my lack of money.

I had enough money for gas. I had counted on G-man to pay half of the bills for the trip. When he bowed out early for a lady, I had to buy all of the gas and other expenses for the rest of the trip. Fortunately, I had his tickets to sell. That helped a little bit, but not much.

I knew I would be arriving in New York City without any kind of knowledge about how to use the train or subway system and knew I didn't have enough money to pay for a cab or possibly the other two transportation systems.

It was too much for me. I had my Rand McNally atlas on my lap and I guided myself to the sports complex in New Jersey on the western side of the Hudson River.

The Grateful Dead concert would be at Giants stadium at the Meadowlands Sports Complex the following evening. I figured my best bet was to pull into the motel parking lot next to the stadium and hole up for a day in the back of my Jimmy until the parking lots opened at the Meadowlands the next day.

The security in the parking lot had other thoughts. I was hassled for sitting in the back of my Jimmy, eating a bologna sandwich and drinking water and reading a book and waiting to fall asleep, so that I could drive across the street the next day to the parking lot in order to attend the concert the next night.

Security didn't have any helpful suggestions about where I should stay for free in the New York City area or any helpful hints about how to navigate the Big Apple with my small town naïveté and empty pocketbook. So, I did the only sensible thing and drove away from New York City.

I didn't drive far. I headed south into a heavily wooded area along the New Jersey Turnpike. I pulled into a small town, Jamesville. I was lost and overwhelmed and looking for a nice side street where I might not get hassled while I slept. I found what looked like a small town bar, walked in, ordered a beer, and asked the bartender where a good place would be to simply pull up and sleep for the night.

That was way out of my comfort zone. I usually wouldn't approach a stranger in New Jersey or New York or wherever the hell I was in a bar and just strike up a conversation. I had probably never been in a bar by myself in my life, but I needed a place to park and did not want to get hassled.

I still had a little LSD and a little marijuana on me, which was also way out of character for me, and certainly did not need to find trouble with the law so far from home. The bartender didn't really look like trouble. He looked a lot like Lou Reed. He was a big fellow with a wavy perm and crazy eyes behind square glasses.

He spoke in a classic accent from that area and warmed up to me once I told him I was from South Dakota and looking for a place to stay before heading to the Grateful Dead concert the next night. He told me that he was a Deadhead and used to go to all the shows.

After I had a beer or two and he sensed that I was pretty innocent and harmless to him, he really heated up and told me that he had actually just spent the last five or 10 years in jail for selling acid at Dead shows. He used to make his living selling drugs. At his final concert, though, he was busted by the cops and had to eat 100 tabs of acid at once and he woke up in a jail cell after several days of a very bad, very long, very strange trip. It cost him several years of his life in prison and he hadn't been to a Dead show since. He was straightening his life out while living with his mom nearby.

He offered to have me park my Jimmy in his mom's driveway if I was willing to wait until he closed the bar for the night. A safe haven sounded good to me and I followed him to his mom's house after he turned out the lights in the bar for the night.

I followed him a short ways and pulled up in the driveway next to the house and I could hear him inside through the screens on a warm summer night telling his mom that I was a good guy and that I was from South Dakota. She must've doubted him because he seemed insistent and repeated it over and over.

The next morning, he came to my Jimmy and asked if he could have a ride to the show. He thought it might be interesting to see what the scene looked like after so many years. I gave him my extra ticket for letting me stay at his place and for showing me where I could camp after the show at Cheesequake State Park. It was just south of New York City and not too far from his home.

That day, we drove towards New York City on the Garden State Parkway. We ended up at the Meadowlands parking lot and said our fond farewells (in my case, good riddances). He said that he would find a way back to his house afterwards and I didn't expect to see him again. He had a lot more experience with a lot more drugs and a lot more street knowledge than I had or ever wanted, even now.

I was thankful that he helped me out, but we didn't need to spend any more time together. He wasn't my type. I hung out in the parking lot that day and commingled with the biggest crowd and parking lot scene I had ever witnessed. The walking lanes between parked cars were packed with vendors and it was often hard to move.

At some point that afternoon I was walking one way down one makeshift street bazaar and I recognized a voice out of the cacophony of sounds coming from the adjacent bazaar street. It was familiar somehow, but I didn't know anyone in that neck of the woods. It was calling "acid, acid, anyone got any acid?" I searched around and could see what looked like Lou Reed's head above the throngs of people.

I avoided him and silently wished him the best now that he had apparently jumped back into the drug selling game. I am pretty sure he sold or lost the ticket I gave him because he was not in the reserved seat that G-man would have occupied when I was inside Giants stadium for the show later that evening.

Too bad for him. They were primo seats. I like to think that the Grateful Dead ticket service set G-man and me up with the best seats at our shows. They knew we were from North Dakota and wanted the kids from the sticks to have a good experience. Again, that was probably naïve thinking at that age, but I was in the 13th row, dead-center in a 90,000 capacity stadium, and it was full.

So was my head. I had dropped acid an hour or two before the show was to begin. Sting was opening for the Grateful Dead at the larger stadium shows and tonight was the first show where he would play. I loved his first band, The Police, and I loved Sting. After all, he was a fellow bass player and had a killer band. I had been looking forward to seeing him and was hoping that I wouldn't have the same experience that I had the summer before with the Steve Miller band.

It wouldn't be the same. I had more experience with LSD under my belt and, even flying solo, I knew better what to expect. I floated into the show and saw Sting and his band put on a stellar performance and Jerry came out and played one song with them. Then, the stadium filled and it was time for the main event.

This was my first show by myself with them and it was outstanding. Even in the midst of that many people, I felt completely secure in my trip and in the music. The boys played Stella Blue at the end of the night and sent the crowd drifting in a mellow haze back into the Meadowlands parking lot.

I found my car, which was actually trickier than you might think, with a head full of psychedelics and that many vehicles. I needed to get to Cheesequake State Park, but when I got behind the wheel, I realized I was still tripping very hard on acid. First of all, I worried that I would get arrested for driving while my brain was on Pluto. Second of all, I didn't seem to understand what a motor vehicle was.

I was actually able to navigate, thanks in part to a concert tape coming from my speakers. I wasn't prepared for the other problem, though. I pulled up at a toll booth in a line of cars to get on the New Jersey Turnpike and I did not have the correct change for the automated toll booth. I didn't have much time to make a decision, either, so I panicked and drove around the barrier. I would have been glad to pay. I just didn't have the right change. I'm not sure I recognized money as currency, either.

I probably should still be in a New York or New Jersey prison but, somehow I was flying south through the swimming lights and painted lines along the freeway with the Grateful Dead cranked on the stereo, living my best life. I arrived at Cheesequake late that night and it was the prettiest place I had ever seen. It still was the next day when I got high and walked around and met all of the trees.

The next day, the Dead were headed to Detroit, and so was I. I departed New York state and drove across Pennsylvania in a rainstorm. Luckily, I met some fellow Deadheads at a rest stop early on in the trip. They offered me some of their joint and I got extremely high and had one of the best drives of my life through the forested interstates of Pennsylvania with, you guessed it, the Grateful Dead blaring on my stereo.

It was bliss. The weed, the music, and the people I was meeting were just too much fun. I camped somewhere at a rest area south of Detroit and tried reading some of Gravity's Rainbow by Thomas Pynchon. It is still the only book that I ever began that I was unable to finish. I tried.

I met some people in Detroit who suggested that I drive to a lake where Heads would be gathering on the day of the show. I hung out there and I have recollections of scattered groups of Deadheads hanging out and partying and smoking grass and maybe skinny-dipping, or maybe that's just what I wanted them to be doing and that was idyllic in my mind. I honestly can't remember if that part actually happened.

After Detroit, it was on to Columbus Ohio. Once again, I arrived the day before the show and was able to scout around the Ohio State campus. I went to the Shoe, the university football field, one of the biggest in the nation, and paid homage to one of my heroes, Archie Griffin. He was a Heisman Trophy-winning running back for the Buckeyes who went on to play for the Cincinnati Bengals. I went to the basketball court on campus to see where John Havlicek and Jerry Lucas had played and where the "golden bear" Jack Nicklaus had played golf in college.

The actual concert was outside of Columbus near a small town called Hebron, Ohio at Buckeye Lake – essentially an amphitheater out in the middle of a field. I had a ticket for that night, but ended up selling it in order to make sure that I had enough money to pay for gas to get back home when the tour ended in a couple of weeks. I hung out in the parking lot all day and began to notice a little bit of the seedier part of the Dead world.

Since I wasn't able to go into the show, I listened to it from outside and it was really difficult to hear because you couldn't get close enough to the stadium for satisfactory sound clarity. So, I wandered around the lot and the field and discovered that the world outside of the show is vastly different than the world inside.

While the show was raging in the amphitheater, drugs were still being sold, and not just psychedelics and marijuana — hard drugs, very damaging and addictive. Alcohol use was out of hand and made all of these problems worse. People were still panhandling, leaving trash all over the place, and partying hard without any regard for the fact that there was a band there. I had to witness all of the things that I was against–these weren't the Deadheads I wanted to be around.

A young woman became incensed with me when she hustled me for spare change and I asked if I could have hers because I didn't have any money to get to the next show, either. She told me I was an asshole. I didn't understand how she could ask for money, but I wasn't allowed to. It still doesn't make any sense to me.

After the Ohio show, I drove to Kentucky for the next stop on tour and spent a few days with my dad's best friend from high school and his college roommate, Mike Goldhammer. He and his two young sons, Benjamin and Christopher, squired me around Louisville. We toured the Kentucky Derby grounds at Churchill Downs and visited the Louisville slugger bat factory. Most importantly, though, I was able to spend some time with one of my dad's best friends, connect with him and learn more about my dad.

One of my friends from South Dakota also came to Louisville to attend the Dead show with me at Freedom Hall. It was his first Grateful Dead show. He loved it, so he traveled along to Chicago to see the Dead play at Soldier Field, which I was doing for the second year in a row.

We camped outside of Chicago at Rockford State Park and rented canoes the day before the show. As we were pulling up to shoreline, he slipped a little in the canoe, lost his balance, and stepped with a foot overboard, landing on the rocky bottom of the lake. When he pulled his foot out of the water his big toe was perpendicular to the rest of his foot. We took him to a doctor and they numbed him up, snapped his toe back into place and gave him a brace. It was not ideal, but he was okay.

We went to Soldier Field the next night and my friend clumsily limped around the parking lot, amazed by the spectacle. He had never taken LSD before and this was to be his first time. We dropped before the show. It went much better finding seats than it had the year before, when I sat in every seat in the place before settling on what was possibly my reserved seat, a la Goldilocks finding the right chair, porridge, and bed. We had great seats, down on the floor, directly in front of Bob Weir at center stage.

A thunderstorm blew in and drenched us for most of the show. Also, the Chicago Bulls were playing in the NBA championship and the network broadcast kept cutting through the Dead's music. They played the game at halftime on the big screens. It was a surreal experience seeing the Dead interwoven with Michael Jordan and Charles Barkley – a horrible juxtaposition if there ever was one.

We were soaked. The rain wouldn't let up. We both had heads full of acid and he had a broken toe, but managed to dance on one foot. It was freakish to hear Marv Albert's voice come out of the speakers at a Grateful Dead concert. It was an excellent time.

My friend had a ticket next to me at the show, but I still had G-man's extra ticket, which I sold to someone in the parking lot. She actually sat with us during the show and her name was Ralph's Mom. She was as high as we were and down to have fun with us. After the show, everything was too soaked to try to camp at Rockford again, so she offered to let us stay at her place in Chicago.

I remember following her vehicle on the Dan Ryan Expressway that night. It was 2:00 in the morning and we were listening to the Dead on the car stereo and I knew life couldn't get any better. We slumbered in the wee hours with the Grateful Dead singing out of her home stereo and slept late into the next morning.

Ralph's Mom was familiar with the city and took us to a Cubs game – great seats at Wrigley Field behind home plate. We were high as kites, still coming down from the night before and full of the weed we had smoked before we went to the ballpark. She took us out for great food and then to the top of Sears tower. After all that, she took us out to see a Dead cover band. I still couldn't get enough of the music.

Chicago was magical that weekend, partly thanks to her knowledge. I left the Windy City the next day by myself, parting company with my friend. I made it to Rochester, Minnesota, to see my good friend McBuddha, who was working and living there with his parents during the summer.

I had saved one hit of acid for each of us from my travels. We dropped it and walked all over Rochester that night and early morning, staring deeply into rain puddles and being amazed by the shapes of trees and how beautiful the world was.

I ended my hero's journey back in Fargo the next day, a completely changed man. I was not the same person who had left town and school five or six weeks prior. I had a taste of some of the world and it only whet my appetite. I knew I needed to experience more of it. North Dakota was not going to be my permanent home and South Dakota would not be, either.

I needed to be in a bigger place, with deeper ideas and more music and tastier food and pristine camping and weirder people to have as friends and mentors. I was thinking about Portland, Oregon or Austin, Texas, or maybe San Francisco or Boulder, Colorado. Those were the cool places where people were telling me to live when I was on the Dead tour. These were cities where I could be me.

Chapter 14

Adulthood

I wanted a bigger, cooler city but, at that moment I had to buckle down and pay off a debt of service to the state of North Dakota. In exchange to the state for paying for my teaching and research assistantships while I was attending school, I had been mandated to spend several months working at a state facility for developmentally or mentally disabled adults or kids. But there were no openings available for me.

One of my professors explained the situation by saying that "you can't squeeze blood out of a turnip." I had no idea what that meant, but if it meant that I didn't have to pay back my obligation, I was going to include it in my vernacular regularly.

Alas, this professor was able to secure for me a three-month job in Fargo working as a consultant at Friendship, Inc., a facility that helped developmentally disabled adults live and work. I would be writing functional assessment plans for the adults there and getting paid as a consultant until Christmas.

Fall in Fargo was good to me. I met a beautiful woman who worked at Friendship, Inc. on the floor. I must have gained some newfound confidence from my travels with the Grateful Dead because I was able to ask her out and we went on a few dates. She had a young daughter.

In retrospect, we had very little in common. I had just completed my master's program and was getting ready to set sail and begin a career. I was knee-deep in music and the Grateful Dead and books and mind-altering substances, mostly all at the same time.

She did not have an education and had not been exposed to any of my music or the experiences I had with psychedelics or any of the books I had read. She professed to like me, though, and was willing to do all sorts of things with me that I liked to do.

I was already planning my exit from Fargo in December, however. I had decided to move to Austin, Texas to see what the world had to offer in terms of music, food, art, outdoors, and new ideas. My buddy Schoeny had already made up his mind that he would move from Houston over to Austin when I came down to Texas and we would take the town by storm.

It wasn't a very good stage in life to get into a relationship with a woman from Fargo with a kid, but I was open to possibilities at that point in my life. I was ready to go all in and see what might happen. Then, she disappeared. Not forever. Just for a weekend.

It threw me for a loop because we were supposed to hang out that weekend and she was just gone. Not answering her phone. Not at her apartment. No trace of her or her child. At the end of the weekend she reappeared and apologized, saying she had something she needed to take care of.

She referred to some kind of dancing thing that she had mentioned at one time. It had to do with bikinis and baby oil and winning a contest. It was super sketchy, but I could believe it. She was definitely a looker. In hindsight, though, I wonder if she may have been a hooker. Or at least a pole dancer. The bottom line was that I had no idea. As usual with women, I was in over my head.

Uncertain of exactly what to do when she resurfaced, I doubled down on the relationship and invited her to move with me to Austin to see where we were headed. It seemed like the right thing to do at the time. She said she was game.

By the next day, I had come to my senses, decided that it wasn't the right thing to do, that it was crazy, and that I wasn't going to speak to her again. It must have worked out for her that way too because I don't think we ever did. Speak to each other again, that is.

I have to say it worked out great for me in the end. For her as well. That would have been disastrous. Tragedy narrowly averted.

Chapter 15

Orange Sunshine

In December of that year, it was time for Schoeny and one of our good buddies from Pierre, Jonny Ballgame, to get on the bus. Neither of them had experienced the Grateful Dead live yet and were chomping at the bit to join the circus. We made plans to travel to San Francisco in December, after I was done with my consulting job in Fargo, to see three nights of the Grateful Dead on their home court at the Oakland Arena.

Schoeny quit the Mattress Firm and moved back to his parents' house in Pierre around Thanksgiving. I finished my consulting job and went home to Pierre for Thanksgiving.

Schoeny returned with me to Fargo after Thanksgiving to pack up my belongings for my final trip south across the Dakota border. We were going to hang out in Fargo for a week, smoke some weed and drink some good beer. We started the party on the way to Fargo after Thanksgiving in the aftermath of a massive snowstorm. The ditches were waist high in snow.

Upon returning from my Dead tour in the summer, I had traded in my 1988 GMC Jimmy. Well, to be fair, I sold it back to my dad, who bought it for me in the first place back in the summer of 1989 when it was only a year old. I had, and have, really good parents.

I sold it because I had my eyes on my buddy McBuddha's 1980 Volkswagen Vanagon. It was orange. That was the color of both the paint job and the rust. The only sticking point with the sale was that it didn't have an engine. I want to say I bought the van for $400 and had a rebuilt engine put in for $4000, but can't remember precisely.

In hindsight, I know with certainty that I got screwed on the deal. It was shit from the first day I owned it until the last day, when it died on I-90 near the Columbia River gorge in Washington state for the great friend/sucker who bought it from me. I'm still sorry about your luck, Metzlahff.

But, in the beginning, buying the van seemed like the right thing to do. I rode a bus from Fargo to Minneapolis on a fall Saturday morning to collect it in Rochester and I drove it back to Fargo the next day.

On that Sunday morning, I was making my way up the busiest street in Fargo. It was several lanes wide, but was relatively quiet because, as I said, it was Sunday morning.

I was in my element in the van, marching my steed like a conquering hero, rolling back into the fort with bootie from the battle. I was wearing Birkenstock sandals from my Dead tour, Guatemalan pants and a Guatemalan Rastafarian yarn hat. I halted only at the gates of dawn, I took no prisoners, and... well, followed all traffic laws and stopped at red lights.

When one red in particular turned green, I pressed the accelerator with my right foot and the pin snapped off underneath the pedal, leaving the pedal lying limply against the floor. My prized Sunshine Daydream van had no way to ambulate.

I must have been quite a sorry sight pushing my van up the street on Sunday morning in my hippie regalia. I have no idea how I made arrangements to get back to my apartment or to have the car towed. I probably should have abandoned the old girl at the light. It was definitely a harbinger of things to come for my life with Sunshine.

I think the gal I dated that fall was not looking for a life with the hippie pushing his dream van up University avenue. I think she was looking for a fellow who drove a Mercedes-Benz or Iroc Z and made a lot of money and could support her and her stripping habit, or whatever it was that she did. Anyway, I digress. Back to moving out of Fargo...

Schoeny and I were very high on our drive up Interstate 29 to Fargo in the post-Thanksgiving blizzard. Sunshine Daydream ferried us along at about 35 miles per hour. Shortly after we crossed the border into North Dakota, I lost control of the van on the ice and snowpack. We spun a few times and landed softly in the ditch. Not so softly, though, that we weren't completely stuck.

Sunshine wasn't a practical winter vehicle and I doubt that we were dressed appropriately for the weather or winter in general. But it made for a great story as we rode in a tow truck with a couple of guys who came down from Fargo to haul the van the rest of the way. I probably missed another opportunity to abandon the old girl in the ditch that day.

Chapter 16

Knockin' On the Golden Door

We said goodbye to North Dakota and made it back to Pierre a week or so later. We left for the Grateful Dead pre-Christmas west coast run with our friend Jonny in Schoeny's white Oldsmobile Cutlass Supreme, his family's pop-up camper in tow.

I had been ill just before the trip and was still feeling the effects when we departed. I was hoping to be healthy by the time we arrived in San Francisco and were in front of the Grateful Dead. Schoeny and Jonny, feeling fine, were good and high before we departed from Fort Pierre that evening.

I sat in the back seat trying to sleep and nurse myself back to health on the 24-hour drive. I listened to them marvel about the night sky as we drove through the dark – across Nebraska and into Wyoming, through Cheyenne and Laramie, then across the Rockies, which were packed with snow.

It was either snowing or had just snowed for much of the trip. We had a couple near misses with low fuel and sketchy roads. Our camper looked like it was doing a crab walk much of the time as it skittered back and forth across the icy roads, both car and camper unfit for such conditions.

But we were on a mission to behold the Grateful Dead and nothing was going to stop our trip or dampen our spirits. Everything just had to work out.

We witnessed an alpine sunrise as we snaked over the Wasatch mountains into Salt Lake City and the Great Salt Lake Basin. As we made our way across the salt flats, the Great Salt Lake on the right, I decided that I was feeling somewhat better. It was time for me to join the party and smoke a little grass with the boys.

Almost immediately after smoking, a highway patrolman pulled up behind our car and followed us for what seemed like eons. It was extremely tense for me in the backseat as I listened to the experimental feedback on Live Dead from 1968 and tried to get on top of the high from the massive amount of marijuana I had just ingested.

I kept warning the other two that we were going to get busted, but they just kept laughing and telling me there was no chance. They were there to party and this was just another fun time and good story for them. Paranoia will destroy ya.

The cop eventually hit an off-ramp or disappeared or dissolved as a figment of my imagination. We arrived in San Francisco late that evening, after weaving our way across the snow-covered Sierra Nevada mountains between Reno and Sacramento. I believe it was snowing and there were flashing lights warning us to chain our tires, but we had no chains. We made our way the best we could, sliding sideways up and over the pass.

I had visions of becoming the Donner party and resorting to cannibalism if we ended up sliding off the road after coming this far on our pilgrimage. But somehow we ended up in San Francisco. Actually, we ended up in the Samuel Taylor State Park and redwoods in Marin County, north of San Francisco Bay. We somehow had the foresight to reserve a place to stay. Our campsite was in the middle of the largest redwoods I have ever seen. They were massive and would be our walls and ceiling for the next few days.

On the first day in our temporary home, we all took some Orange Sunshine that we had scored from our friend Redfeather back in Pierre. We were going to trip and play around in the trees all day and maybe night. An hour or so after we dropped the acid, we were wandering deep in the forest and the drug hit. I immediately knew things were going to be dicey as I was hit with a terror like no other I had ever felt.

I had experienced anxiety before, certainly. I knew well the first rush of LSD and the overwhelming sensations that it brought before settling into something more manageable. This feeling I was having was something entirely different. This was sheer terror – everything in my brain was telling me I couldn't escape and it was going to last forever.

Even the trees were frightening, and Schoeny and Jonny's enthusiasm was not matching my experience. They were completely on top of the trip and having the time of their lives.

They were leaping from tree to tree, walking over felled trees 15 to 20 feet above the forest floor, screaming at the top of their lungs about how they were one with the forest and the connection of all things. Their minds were being blown. Mine was in a never-ending horror movie loop. I felt helpless.

In my saner moments, or all the moments in my life except for those that occurred that day, I would have been right with them in sheer bliss. That day, though, they were scaring me to death because I couldn't approach their state. I was losing my mind and there was no way it was coming back. I had an incredible sense of isolation. I couldn't connect with anything. Not with my best friends, not with nature, and certainly not with myself.

This lasted the entire afternoon and evening, but it might as well have lasted for a lifetime. I finally managed to get on top of the drug in the middle of the night, maybe by midnight. We sat around a fire at the campsite and Schoeny and I played our guitars. The music was soothing and was finally something to which I could relate. I was struggling mightily to make the best of this acid trip, but I was shaken to the core.

At one point, Jonny put lighter fluid on the fire. I'm not sure if it was while he was building it or if he was doing it just for kicks. It may have been acid vision, but I watched it raise an inferno as high as the treetops in the redwoods. It was a literal explosion. It blew Jonny backwards through the air and he tumbled onto the ground.

I thought Jonny and Schoeny might die from a fit of laughter. I may have even thought it was funny, too, if I hadn't just been a puddle – a mere catatonic remnant of the day's psychedelic blitzkrieg.

All of my other acid trips had answered questions. This one did nothing but raise them.

We went to bed at some point in the camper, but didn't sleep much because it was December and freezing in the redwoods of northern California. Also, because raccoons kept crawling up and slipping into our camper between the door and canvas cover. They were after food and we were constantly shooing them away. We couldn't sleep because we had to be on guard for beady eyes glowing in the dark above the door.

At that age, fortunately, not getting much sleep was part of the adventure. We were unfazed and had our energy back, glowing with the prospect of seeing the Grateful Dead later that day.

I still wasn't feeling that great the day of the first Dead show in the three-night run. It could have been because of the illness I was still recovering from when we left, or it might have been because I was still reeling from the day in the woods that went awry. Either way, I didn't quite have the same energy and enthusiasm the other two guys had in the parking lot bazaar the day of the show.

That didn't stop me from trying to make things right by dropping part of another tab of acid for the first show. Just half for me, please. And not Orange Sunshine, please and thank you. The episode in the woods the day before shook me.

My buddies were absolutely flying and didn't have my newfound fear of LSD. Make it a double, barkeep. Heavy on the lysergic. They were on cloud nine and reminded me of myself during my first Dead show in Chicago when I finally got on top of the acid.

On this night, in the dead of a bay area winter, the entire Oakland Arena lifted off the ground and spun around in the air for some time during the Drums and Space portion of the show in the second set. The logical mind says that buildings that big don't float, but there is no doubt about it happening. The entire arena felt it, and the three of us certainly rose and spun. I have since gone back and listened to audio from that night and it is actually possible to tell exactly when it began to lift off.

The Dead were entirely capable of levitating buildings. After all, they were playing Fire On the Mountain at the Portland Memorial Coliseum in Oregon when Mount St. Helens erupted. They were capable of creating meteorological events while playing Cold Rain and Snow, Looks Like Rain, Weather Report Suite, and so many other songs with weather references, so why not believe they could rip buildings from their foundations and gently place them back down after everyone had enjoyed the ride?

We left the concert that night floating high and somehow navigated the winding roads through the forest back to our campsite on auto pilot. I think somebody was at the wheel of the Cutlass, but how they avoided all of those redwood trees is still a mystery to me.

I still wasn't feeling up to par and thankfully had the sense to stay sober the second night. For a change of pace, we sat directly behind the band and I really wasn't of a mind to have a great time. The other two dropped acid and were just as into it as they were the night before.

Going into the third night in row, I had a fever and chills and body aches and probably full-on influenza. I hadn't come this far to miss the Grateful Dead, though, and the boys basically carried me into the arena and I sat in my chair and attempted to enjoy the show, butt on chair. Following the encore that night, they carried me out to the car, wrapped me in blankets and drove me back to the campground. We got there and I remained in the car in my cocoon while they slept in the camper. I didn't want to move, but I couldn't have if I'd wanted to.

The next morning, they hooked the camper to the Cutlass and we lit out for Christmas in Pierre. In the parking lot before one of the shows, they had bought a sheet (100 tabs of acid), new pipes, weed and California white sage that had a smell they were enamored with. They stayed incredibly elevated all the way back to South Dakota.

Early on, they discovered that they were building tolerance and the acid was no longer doing what it was supposed to do with one hit. They kept taking five more every half hour or so until they were up to 25 or 30.

I lost count from the backseat, but I listened and smelled as they continued to light up the weed pipe in order to enhance the LSD and took uppers in order to stay awake and stay on top of the high.

The car was filled with smoke for the entire 24 hour drive, either from marijuana or from the white sage, which is still hard for me to smell to this day because it is connected to my state on the drive home.

When we arrived in our hometown late in the afternoon on the winter solstice, they dumped me inside the front door of my parent's house. I was still incredibly sick. It took me a long time to recover from that trip, but I eventually did, just like I had with every other illness in my life. I was fairly healthy again by the new year and, thankfully, didn't seem to be permanently damaged from the redwoods acid trip.

Chapter 17

Wanted Man in Texas

In January, I loaded my belongings into Sunshine Daydream and made tracks for Texas, where Mark had already arrived and secured an apartment in a low-income, mostly Latino neighborhood in Austin. He already had a job by the time I arrived, too. Well...a job of sorts.

He signed on to work for Greenpeace and it didn't technically pay. Daily, he would go to the headquarters downtown in his professional work attire–a yarn hat, yarn sandals and shorts, as well as (usually) a Grateful Dead shirt. It was a far cry from the dress shirt, tie and slacks he donned at The Mattress Firm over in Houston the year before. He had also begun to grow his hair and was sporting a beard.

He and the other Greenpeace volunteers, who closely resembled him in dress and mannerisms, would meet in their tiny office in downtown Austin every day. They would blaze up on marijuana and be assigned to different sections of the city. They knocked on doors to talk about how to save the environment with affluent hill country people. More likely than not, the door would be slammed in their faces.

Meanwhile, I was putting on a suit jacket and tie with mandatory navy blue slacks every day to work at United Video as an assistant sales manager. This impressive title meant I would begin my days by calling people who had VHS tapes that were overdue. I started each morning calling the most egregious offenders.

I would call Mrs. Gonzalez, who had a copy of Blood In, Blood Out that was overdue by 35 days. Then came Mr. Rodriguez, who had a copy of Menace II Society that was overdue by 32 days. On I went, down the list, trying to track down videotapes people had forgotten to return to my store. They mostly hung up on me. The rest of the day, I checked out video tapes to customers.

I would repeat the same cycle the next day and the next, the only difference being that Blood In, Blood Out was now another day overdue. Menace II Society wasn't magically returned either, despite my diligence and cajoling. I have yet to watch either film, even though they occupied so much of my time in Austin.

My boss was an asshole and my coworkers felt the same way about him. About two months into the job, three of us met for coffee at the McDonald's across the strip mall parking lot from United Video. We all ate a hearty breakfast, had some laughs, then went in and told the boss to take his job and shove it.

We felt extremely empowered and liberated as we drove around the city in my coworker's convertible with the top down, but I needed a job to pay the rent. Lord knows Schoeny wasn't bringing in much income trying to talk about saving whales.

I hoped to find a job in my chosen profession in Austin. After all, I had not gone to that much school and earned my master's degree so I could work in a video store. I applied for a couple of professional counseling jobs and had interviews. My youth and inexperience, social anxiety, and the fact that Austin had the highest number of unemployed advanced degrees in the United States at the time, all conspired against me.

I did temp work for a short stretch and was finally hired as a direct care worker with developmentally disabled adult males. I was running a home in north central Austin with six adult males.

It was the best of times, and it was the worst of times.

The six guys and I became fast friends. I didn't know many people in Austin. Schoeny and I weren't the best (or even good, if I'm honest) at reaching out and meeting people.

We tended to hang out together all the time. Whether it was the paradise of Barton Springs to swim on days we weren't working, or camping on the cliffs overlooking Lake Travis at Pace Bend Park in the hill country west of Austin. We would also go to music shows or just sit in the apartment smoking weed and watching movies or listening to music. We didn't come anywhere near meeting any ladies and we didn't have any other close friends.

Eventually, Schoeny needed a job that paid real money and he was hired by my organization. He supervised a group home for developmentally disabled adult men in south Austin. We would get our guys together for a meet-up on free live music nights down at Lake Travis. We would all dance to the music with thousands of other people sharing in the fun.

The men we worked with were tremendously fun. They had good senses of humor and an understanding of the world that we would never have. I've always had a theory that the developmentally disabled folks I worked with were playing a cosmic joke on the rest of us – really, they were the ones who had the deep insight. My thoughts about it haven't changed to this day.

Schoeny scored a group of fairly easy-going guys. While I loved them like family, my guys were a constant, major struggle. One of them, Michael, was unable to care for himself, or maybe just unwilling, it was hard to tell. He was non-verbal and couldn't share his intentions that way.

Every day, I had to wake him up right away in the morning and force him to shower. I would go in his room and tell him to shower and he would continue to lie in bed.

I would move on to the rest of the guys in their rooms, return to Michael in five minutes and I would make him sit up by physically lifting him.

I would leave and five minutes later, I'd come back and he would still be sitting there. I would stand him up.

I would direct him to take his clothes off and get in the shower and I would leave.

I would come back in five minutes and he would be standing, fully clothed, just as I left him.

I would then take his clothes off and tell him when I came back in five minutes I wanted him in the shower.

I would come back in five minutes and he would be standing in his room, naked and flicking his wiener with the back of his hand.

I would take him by the shoulders and walk him to the bathroom.

I would turn on the shower and tell him that in five minutes I would return and I wanted him in the shower.

I would come back in five minutes and he would be standing in front of the shower, flicking his wiener with the back of his hand.

I would lift him into the shower and I would tell him I was coming back in five minutes and that he needed to put shampoo on his head.

I would come back in five minutes and he would still be standing there in the shower flicking his wiener with the back of his hand.

I would force him under the water and pour shampoo on his head.

I would tell him I was coming back in five minutes and I needed him to be rinsed when I returned.

When I came back in five minutes he was never rinsed.

You get the picture. This was how I began every day at work.

It was exasperating. While I was gone for each of those five minutes, I was scrambling back to the kitchen to cook for the guys. Harold, an old Black man who was extremely tense and constantly agitated, would come by and ask me what I was cooking. I might tell him that I was cooking eggs and sausage and he would scream at me that he "didn't want no eggs and sausage." Then he would begin to pace and continue to yell that he didn't want what I was cooking. Repeatedly.

Stanley Bradford, a muscular Black man in his 30s, would strut around the house, yelling at the top of his lungs "I'm Stanley Bradford" while grinning from ear to ear. He was very happy most of the time, until he was not. When the time came, he was usually mad at Harold.

When Stanley and Harold got mad at each other, look out. They were not to be stopped. They were forces of nature and would scream at the top of their lungs with deep, vicious growls and they would make overtures like they were going to fight each other. Word had it that one of my coworkers found them having anal sex one time, so I think it would be safe to say they had a very complicated relationship.

Then there was Steve, who was low functioning, non-verbal, and preferred his own company. He was a short white guy of indeterminate age with extremely thick toenails. Part of my job description was to clip his toenails. The only problem was, on toenail clipping day, I would approach him with a pair of clippers and he would begin to squeal like a stuck hog.

I certainly didn't want to cause him harm, but my boss expected me to cut his toenails, which I was being paid for. And Steve wasn't letting me anywhere near them. I can still remember his piercing screams as he ran away. It was my job, though.

I don't remember that I was ever able to cut even one of his toenails. I sometimes wonder how long those nails are nowadays. He might even make a run for the Guinness Book of World Records against the lady who has nails that are curled like a rams horn and are several feet long.

Then there was Marcelo, an old Mexican man who just walked around shaking his head because he couldn't believe the chaos. He generally remained above the fray. He was very nice to me and we were able to talk from time to time. I had a lot of respect for him, but I could tell he felt out of place in the home and sometimes his frustration bubbled into anger at the way people were acting around him. He would have fit in well in Schoeny's home of cooperative, higher functioning dudes.

Finally, there was Lorenzo. Lorenzo was a pear-shaped Mexican man about 30 years old. He talked in a high voice and was as sweet as you could possibly imagine. He wasn't the highest functioning, but he was probably the most loving. Until he wasn't.

There was a morning when I had just come out of Michael's bathroom after putting him in the shower and was returning down the hallway to check the eggs with Harold screaming at me that he "didn't want no eggs" and Stanley Bradford strutting around smiling at me and loudly telling us all who he was, over and over. Believe me, I already knew who he was. He was Stanley Bradford.

As I walked down the narrow hallway, I caught a glimpse of movement out of the corner of my eye and wheeled around just in time to see Lorenzo grab a framed picture from the wall and try to brain me with it. I was somehow able to dodge the swing, grab him, and get him into some kind of makeshift submission hold. Looking back, it was basically a ninja move.

I lowered him to the carpet while he scratched and clawed at me and showered me with saliva and squealed and screamed and roared. He became an entirely different person and was not controllable by reason or logic.

This happened more than once. With each episode, once he was subdued and had submitted, the rest of the day he would walk around asking me repeatedly in a high-pitched voice "Scott, why are you mad at me? Why are you mad?" I would just repeat "I'm not mad at you Lorenzo." I wanted to add "for chrissake, even though you tried to smite me with a goddamn picture frame."

Each day, after the shower and breakfast challenges, I would take a half an hour drive down interstate 35 to south Austin with all of the guys in the 15 passenger work van. This was the daily commute so they could make buttons at their factory job Monday through Friday. We would drive 80 miles an hour in bumper-to-bumper traffic during rush hour.

One day, as we sped along on our route to the job site, Lorenzo, who was seated behind me on the bench seat, used his lunchbox cooler as a projectile aimed at my head. After throwing the lunchbox at me, he opened the rear passenger door, and tried to leap onto the interstate at full speed. Somehow, I managed to grasp the back of his t-shirt and stop him from falling to his gruesome death.

I still have visions of his shoes bouncing up and down off of the pavement as we drove at full speed with cars on both sides of us and others behind us. All while moving at 80 MPH. It was harrowing.

I managed to slow down and steer the car onto the shoulder, but he evaded my grasp and jumped over a fence, running into a field. This was not your normal, everyday work commute.

Desperate, I left five adult men with significantly impaired judgement skills on a busy interstate shoulder, went into the field, and approached Lorenzo carefully. I was finally able to coax him back into the van, but he was not able to go to work with his buddies that day.

When the guys had an episode that severe, there was a place they went during the day that they definitely did not want to go. I was never there, but my understanding is that it wasn't too pleasant and they were usually pretty cooperative when they returned to the group home in the evening.

It reminded me of Randle McMurphy in One Flew Over the Cuckoo's Nest when he would return to his floor on the psych ward after having electric shock treatments or his eventual lobotomy.

It didn't take long for the stress of witnessing Lorenzo's near-death and of dealing with the day-to-day antics in the home for me to realize I couldn't stay in that job much longer. I loved the guys, but I was going to end up beating Mike during shower time in the morning, or I was going to get killed when Lorenzo smashed me with the painting or when he killed himself by jumping from the moving van. I might even be fired because I couldn't cut Steve's toenails. I desperately needed a change.

Chapter 18

Homesick

In addition to the job stress, I was tremendously homesick. I couldn't get time off from the job during holidays (or maybe any time), and I didn't have money to travel home even if I did have the time. My younger brother was a sophomore in high school and I was missing all of his high school activities and my family in general.

I didn't want to have regrets about not spending time with my family members while I had the chance, so I was trying to get back to South Dakota. Truthfully, I didn't really want to live in South Dakota, either. It felt like it would be death to ideas and creativity and inspiration. But it was home.

In March of 1994, I turned 25 and celebrated on a cliff overlooking Lake Travis on the Colorado River at Pace Bend campground in the hill country west of Austin. Jonny Ballgame, his girlfriend and his older sister, Sweet Virginia, came to Texas for a visit and to spend my birthday with me.

We had a great time dancing to Grateful Dead concert tapes under the stars and playing our guitars cliffside.

All of them were tripping hard on acid except me. I had my fill in Oakland last December and hadn't quite recovered completely, either physically or maybe psychologically.

Austin was a ways from home. I missed my family. Schoeny and I were 25-year-old men crowding each other in a small apartment, both spatially and metaphysically. Something had to change.

I was burned out the instant I watched Lorenzo try to jump onto the interstate.

My dad mailed a job notice to me from his local paper for a family service counselor opening at St. Joseph's Indian school in Chamberlain, South Dakota. My parents had grown up in Chamberlain and were high school sweethearts there. It was less than 90 miles from my parents and brother in Pierre.

I had two widowed grandmothers there, where they had lived for their entire lives. They were each 77 years old in 1994. I loved them dearly, but didn't know if I wanted to live in the same town in South Dakota with them – especially if that town was Chamberlain, population 2,300.

In pondering a change of scenery, I was mostly considering the Black Hills area and its outdoor possibilities. But, St. Joe's flies their prospective employees in for interviews and it seemed like a good idea to at least see what they had to offer. I would also be able to see my family on their dime, which was a trip I couldn't afford on my own.

I flew home and stayed with my Grandma Woster in Chamberlain while I interviewed at St. Joe's. I discovered that I would not be working a good part of the summer and that I would have two weeks of Christmas break, a week at Thanksgiving, and a week at spring break to explore the world and visit family. I could sate my wanderlust appetite and replant my roots where they had been from the start.

In my time visiting Chamberlain in my youth, I had never visited St. Joseph's. This would be my first time ever seeing the place. I vividly remember steering my grandmother's car onto the campus at St. Joseph's Indian school on a weekday morning.

At the first student residence I passed, I noticed a car in the driveway that had personalized license plates from Ohio with the letters GDTRFB on it. I immediately perceived it as a hopeful sign. I recognized the letters as an abbreviation for the Grateful Dead song Going Down the Road Feeling Bad. It was actually a traditional folk song, but the Dead included it as part of their repertoire from their early days.

Instead of proceeding to human resources and my interview, I pulled over to the curb and rushed into the residence closest to the car. There was a meeting happening at the dining room table and heads and eyebrows raised as I blurted out an apology for interrupting the meeting and inquired about the car parked outside with Dead plates.

A young bearded man seated at the table smiled shyly and responded that it was his. We greeted each other briefly and I moved on. During our short encounter, he had time to explain there were several deadheads who worked at the school from all over the country.

St. Joe's offered me the job a few days after I returned to Austin. I was told by the woman in human resources that the salary would be in the low $20,000s, but she was going to confirm the number and get back to me. She phoned a day later and made me a firm offer of the lowest of the low 20s, $20,000 on the nose. Despite being the lowest offer possible, it was more than I was currently making.

It wasn't much money considering I had a master's degree, but it would allow me to return to South Dakota. I also knew the opportunity would put me in a place where I would be surrounded with some people from all over the country who would share their different perspectives and experiences with me. And, it afforded me the opportunity to travel in the summer and during school year breaks.

My Grateful Dead travel would be possible, as would my outdoor excursions and exposure to different parts of the country, and hopefully the world. Now that I had survived the interview (as one might imagine, I spent the better part of the interview day and the night before having a panic attack), I could stop cutting my hair again and I could grow the ponytail I always wanted. It was likely one of the last times I wore slacks, a tie, and a sport coat as well.

I would fit right in with the hippies at St. Joseph's. They were a minority, though, in conservative Chamberlain. There were probably quite a few people shaking their heads when I pulled up in an orange Volkswagen van for my first day of orientation that year.

Chapter 19

Mystery Illness

I said so long to Schoeny in Texas and to my guys at the group home and arrived in Chamberlain on July 2nd, 1994. I began work after the 4th of July holiday weekend, on July 5th. I had just enough time in July to travel to Indiana and then to Chicago to see the Grateful Dead for three concerts before the school year began.

Schoeny was planning to come to Noblesville, Indiana from Texas with our old friend Ralph's Mom, of 1993 Soldier Field and Chicago fame. She helped me plan to surprise him at the Deer Creek Amphitheater shows there.

I was waiting in the parking lot, which was a massive grassy field, on my bike at Deer Creek when he pulled in with Ralph's mom. He had just taken acid shortly before arriving and he was definitely surprised to see me there. We spent three nights at the concerts, one at Deer Creek and two at Soldier Field.

The two of them enjoyed Jesus hits of acid (his face was literally the face on each tiny square of paper) at the second show in Chicago. It must've been good stuff, because they were certainly over the moon and enjoyed themselves that night at the show. I may have smoked a little marijuana, but I don't remember for sure.

I was not having any luck with mind alteration anymore. I hadn't done much since the previous Christmas and the Bay Area Dead shows and the LSD trip in the redwoods that went awry.

Before I left Austin, Schoeny and I floated the Pedernales River on inner tubes and we took mushrooms, which I hadn't tried before, prior to setting sail.

Once the mushrooms hit, I couldn't get on top of my trip. As was becoming customary, Schoeny was having a blast floating in the water and being amazed by the simplicity of nature. Water, rocks, trees, wow... but not for me.

He marveled at a turtle on the bank of the river and was pointing it out to me, raving that there was something amazing about it. For the life of me, I couldn't figure out why he was so elated because I was terrified and confused. I don't think he knew whether to make fun of me or to worry about me.

With time, I was able to finally get on top of the high but I knew that my experimentation with psychedelics was likely over. A bad trip is not a feeling you want to have in your life and I had experienced it twice now. It wasn't worth it. That was all she wrote for me and psychedelics.

So, when we showed up for the concerts, I was the odd man out and the sober guy. I had some slight nagging wistfulness that I wanted to still be in the game and be a part of what they were experiencing, but it was mitigated by the negative trips. I simply didn't feel good enough about it to partake. I enjoyed the shows, but something was missing that had been there in the 1992-93 concerts for me.

It wasn't the music. That hadn't changed for me. I wasn't just another picky, wizened Deadhead yet. Jerry's health was declining, but I wasn't really noticing and had no premonition that he would be dead in a year.

I wasn't missing the drugs. I could live without them and the drugs that I had been doing occasionally for the past year or so did not have an addictive value to them, so I wasn't physically dependent or withdrawing.

But something was missing. Whatever it was that wasn't there for me, it was definitely there for Schoeny and Ralph's mom, because they had a rip-roaring time.

When I returned from Chicago, I made one last trip for the summer before beginning the week-long staff orientation at St. Joe's. Jonny, his sister Sweet Virginia and I went to western South Dakota to camp in the Badlands on a scorching summer weekend in August.

At 25-years-old, this would be the last time I would ever use marijuana, and it would be my last beer as well.

We hiked and played around in the Badlands, smoked pot and camped for a couple of nights. I saw more stars in the Badlands sky than I have in any other place, at any other time in my life. It was magical.

On the last day, we broke camp and drove Sunshine eastward on Highway 18 across the state. We were smoking on the drive. The two came back to Chamberlain with me to collect their car and drive back to Pierre, where they were both living with their parents at the time.

I went inside my small house to prepare for my first day of orientation the next day. I made Ramen noodles and settled in for the evening. Willie Clearwater pulled up in front of the house with all his belongings crammed into his vehicle and a U-Haul. He was on his way to live in Denver. He was moving there from Sioux Falls and stopped in for a surprise visit.

As we visited, I became more and more nauseous and lightheaded, even disoriented. It became severe enough that I went out into the backyard and forced myself to vomit, leaving my Ramen noodles in the grass. Throwing up didn't help me at all and Willie departed for Colorado later that night, leaving me to suffer by myself.

I spent the entire night in the same state, unable to sleep, desperately unsettled and, quite frankly, terrified. It was completely overwhelming and I had no explanation for why it was happening.

I called in sick the next day and missed my first day of orientation. I proceeded to miss over a week of a two-week orientation, either too sick to work or too busy visiting doctors. I went to visit a general practitioner in Chamberlain and he suggested that I had allergies. I didn't think I had allergies, or anything that benign or understandable or treatable.

It was almost as if I knew immediately – the first night when Willie stopped to visit – that something irreversible and unexplainable was happening to me. And it was completely debilitating.

I knew instantly and with certainty that it wasn't going away. This wasn't a feeling that food or medicine or sleep would help me out of. It wasn't leaving; and it was going to be life-changing.

I vowed that night to never drink or smoke again. I just wanted to feel normal. I also knew that I would never marry or have a family, or possibly even go on a date. There was absolutely no way. I knew I would be lucky to hold a job and I worried I would have to move back in with my parents. All of this hit me like a ton of bricks, just as immovable.

If it seems overly dramatic, trust me, I realize that. All these thoughts were painfully clear to me and I couldn't see around them. I had no perspective. Absolutely none.

Everyone around me was completely supportive – all of my coworkers, family and friends. But they could not understand me. I couldn't understand me. My healthy self couldn't make any sense of my sick self and vice versa.

I had never been a crier, but now I cried often, sometimes because the need was overwhelming and sometimes because I knew I would likely never be the same again. I was crying over a loss that seemed certain, but also inexplicable.

Over the next seven months, I visited countless doctors. I went to see an actual allergist in Rapid City who performed skin tests. I visited an ear, nose and throat specialist to see if I had an inner ear infection that made me lightheaded and disoriented. I went to an optometrist and then an ophthalmologist. I went to a neurologist.

I quickly became despondent and felt helpless. I missed a month to six weeks of work in the first six or seven months at my new job. I felt bad for St. Joseph's taking a chance on me – I was a bad hire.

Even when I did make it to work, I had to force myself to just survive for eight hours; I felt completely ineffective. I would come home at the end of the day and lie on the couch, not moving until the next day when I had to go back to work.

Often, I did not bother to eat. Most times, I did not bother sleeping in my bed. I would just stay on the couch with the television on, staring at shows I never would have dreamed of actually watching. I didn't even like television, I just needed the company of it.

Sometimes my Grandma Gust would leave work at the A&W, which she owned and operated after my grandfather died eight years prior, and deliver a hamburger and a malt, just to make sure I got some food. My Grandma Woster tried as well. They loved me, but couldn't understand my situation. There simply wasn't much they could do to help.

At Christmas, I was so depressed and anxious over the whole thing that I finally tried an antidepressant. That experiment lasted for about 48 hours. I took it just before bedtime and had harrowing nights. I barely slept, lying in bed gripped by a state of panic and paranoia.

The antidepressant just seemed to make everything much worse. At that point, I felt that life was hopeless. I contemplated leaving the world and had a plan. I don't think I would have ever had the courage to follow through with it, though, which only compounded the frustration I was feeling.

Facing life with death as the only viable option is terrifying. There is nothing more frightening. At least, that has been my experience.

By February 1995, I had visited every medical specialist my family and I could think of and had no definitive conclusions. I made up my mind to go to either the Mayo Clinic in Rochester, Minnesota or the University of Minnesota, the top medical facilities in the region. With my nurse mom, who had been with me every step of the way during doctor visits, I would present my symptoms and stay until they could find an answer.

I had no clue how to navigate that system and simply could not have done so by myself, given my state. I was lucky to make it to work and function each day and sometimes I couldn't even do that.

That was my life in February 1995. My grandma had gone on a week-long trip to Colorado to visit my uncles and their families. When she left, I went to her house for a change of scenery. I couldn't tolerate staring at the same walls of my house and being reminded of my sickness, so I went and looked at her walls for the next six days.

I put a sleeping bag in front of her TV on a Tuesday night (Valentine's Day, I remember) and my health became bad enough that I missed work on Wednesday, Thursday and Friday. I didn't really move from that spot on the floor for a few days, except for trips to the bathroom. I likely wasn't eating much, if at all.

On Sunday, my parents came to town to see me, ostensibly to talk about our next step, which would likely be a visit to Mayo Clinic. They arrived at my grandma's house in the mid-afternoon and sat me down on the couch. They let me know that my dad had cancer and was having surgery in a few weeks. My mom had to focus all her attention on him at that point.

They were both working full-time jobs, of course. My brother was a junior in high school and still at home. They had their hands full. I had tremendous guilt about bothering them with my problems. I knew precisely how difficult my situation was making their lives.

They apologized that they wouldn't be able to take me to Mayo until after dad had recovered from surgery. I was devastated for him and also for me. I sobbed unceasingly and clung to my dad. I was sad and afraid because of his illness. I also knew I had no hope of getting any relief for mine.

I was crumbling. I knew that if something happened to my dad, I wouldn't be able to deal with it. If I lost a parent while I felt like I did, I would absolutely unravel.

In a complete act of desperation, I loaded up my van the next day, a Monday, and drove to Rochester alone. I presented myself at the emergency room to seek answers. They directed me to come to the clinic the next morning and check in at the front desk to get an appointment.

I discovered at the front desk that they didn't have any walk-ins available, which I presumed would be the case. They informed me that I would have to wait for a cancellation. I would have to stay in town and come to the waiting room each day. They would call my name when – and if – they had a cancellation.

I found a cheap motel room and diligently showed up at Mayo clinic as instructed on Tuesday, Wednesday, Thursday, and Friday. Finally, on Friday, they called my name. I met with a general practitioner who made me appointments for the next week from Monday through Friday with all the specialists they had there.

She scheduled a follow-up meeting with her for next Friday to provide me with answers. In the meantime, she sent me to the Barnes & Noble bookstore across the street. She suggested that I acquire copies of books about Chronic Fatigue Syndrome.

I hadn't been able to read since the previous August. The typed words would bounce up and down. It was like reading through a screen door, so it was a particularly easy choice to avoid books. But, armed with new purpose, I forced myself to try reading the Chronic Fatigue books. I isolated myself in my room with the tv on. What else was I going to do?

One night, I tried a movie and went to see Pulp Fiction. I was paranoid the whole time and my brain was not functioning well enough to follow the plot. A few years later, when I was healthier, I saw the movie again and realized it was pure genius. It's still a favorite of mine, despite the disturbing evening in the Rochester theater. Or, maybe because of that evening in the Rochester theatre. It's possible that the memory of that night represents a new level of recovery for me.

I spent the entire weekend in the motel room reading books on chronic fatigue and the subject resonated with me. The developing theme was that patients had no concrete answers to a sickness that comes out of nowhere and refuses to get better.

After a week of tests and meetings daily with multiple Mayo specialists, my general practitioner and I met again on a Friday afternoon. She diagnosed me with Chronic Fatigue Immune Dysfunction Syndrome and prescribed me a tricyclic antidepressant, Pamelor.

She validated my concerns about the previous antidepressant I had taken and noted that it was from a different classification of antidepressant medications. I knew all of that in theory because I had studied it in graduate school and many of my practicum patients were prescribed these pills. But, in practice, I was scared to death to take another one due to my previous experience.

My doctor instructed me to begin with the absolute minimum dosage of 10 mg for a week, then to bump to 20 mg for a week, then to bump to 30 mg for a week, then to 40 mg for a week, and finally to 50 mg for a week. This "maximum dose" for me, 50 mg, was still only a third of the dose she would normally prescribe for someone with clinical depression.

The goal was to gradually increase my dose so I could tolerate the medication in baby steps. I was slightly embarrassed, but desperation didn't let me feel that way for long. I was discharged from Mayo after meeting with her on that Friday. I bawled my way through the eight hour drive back to my parents' house. I felt I had little more to go on than I had when I left Chamberlain almost two weeks ago, after spending a week on my grandma's floor.

In Pierre, I sat at my parents' dinner table and cried while mom assured me they would take care of me if necessary and do whatever they needed to do, including moving me back into their house. My dad just kept encouraging me, telling me that I didn't need to come back to live with them. He told me that I was going to survive and that I just needed to keep pushing. This wasn't said harshly, and it wasn't taken harshly. I just think he–both of them, really– knew I would feel an overwhelming sense of failure to be back with them. That would be worse than whatever awaited me on my own.

On Sunday, I cried my way back to Chamberlain in Orange Sunshine and into the job I hadn't worked for the past two-and-a-half weeks. It was also the job I had missed fully one third of in my first six months of employment. It was sheer desperation that forced me to find a way to put one foot in front of the other each day at work.

From reading my Chronic Fatigue books, it was clear that many of the patients in the books were attempting to do the same thing. They were just trying to survive. To exist. Some were able to manage by simply forcing themselves to move forward. Some were not. Some were unable to work for years. Some got sick and then miraculously recovered their health six months later, a year later, five years later, 10 years, 20 years later. Some never recovered.

The more I read about Chronic Fatigue, which is all I wanted to read at that point because it was the only thing I could connect with, the more I found out about different cures and treatments. Some were standard medicine and some alternative, but some people were able to find combinations to nurse themselves back to health. I researched many, tried some and didn't bother with others.

I'd obsessively begun to keep a journal in order to log my symptoms and giving each day a subjective rating from 1-10. I was looking for order and structure to the illness, but there was none to be found. My health settled into an indeterminable pattern: a week of barely being able to function would be followed by a week of relatively good health, followed by a month of terrible days, followed by three days of good. No pattern made sense and nothing I did seemed to affect it.

With chronic fatigue, a hallmark symptom is intense lack of energy following exertion. As a result, I had been avoiding asserting myself physically for the last eight months. For about a year after my trip to the Mayo Clinic, I attempted to actively rest and take care of myself. Going to work was about all the exertion I could manage.

I took the prescribed tricyclic medication, but when I reached 30 or 40 mg, I began to have what felt like paranoia and my symptoms seemingly worsened. My Mayo doctor backed me off to 10 to 20 mg if I could tolerate it, which I could.

She again stressed that she was not treating me for depression, but instead was treating me for sleep difficulty. Her theory was that, if I slept better, the illness would improve. To me, the theory was sound, but it didn't seem to make much of a difference in my world.

It may have made a slight difference, or there may have been a placebo effect that I was getting something positive from my 10 to 20 mg of Pamelor. There's not a doctor around that would tell me I was really getting a true effect from that small dose, but my mind had convinced me that it might be helping slightly, so I clung to that.

A year after my Mayo trip, in 1996, I began to do very mild workouts, mostly weight training and bike riding. Over time, I found that these didn't seem to make me feel any worse than I was going to anyway. That doesn't mean they weren't difficult to complete, it just means they likely weren't hurting me.

By 1997 or 1998, I was back to working myself to exhaustion in a good way – on the mountain bike, in the weight room and playing basketball. At times, I suffered for it later, but I think it was worth it for my overall emotional stability. Ever since, I have been dependent upon some type of daily work out.

I had always been active and engaged in athletic activities, but now it was absolutely imperative to my wellbeing. Quite possibly, I literally needed it to stay alive, more so from a mental and emotional health perspective.

This pattern of unpredictable waxing and waning health continued for the next 10 years or so. I had some normal days and I had some awful days. During that time, I didn't date. I didn't think about being in a relationship. I couldn't imagine bringing another person into my world of ever-changing health patterns. Also, I wasn't remotely interested in one-night stands or meeting women at bars. I had no desire for that kind of ugliness anymore.

I did not want to date anyone that I wasn't going to make a lifelong commitment to. This was problematic because I had decided that I would never be able to make a lifelong commitment to anyone due to the illness. I knew that I would be a lifelong bachelor and I had peace with that, but did not have peace with the unpredictable nature of Chronic Fatigue Syndrome.

I did some things with friends occasionally, visited my parents and spent time with close family, but that was the extent of my social engagements. I was still completely sober and didn't even drink so much as a beer. I was terrified of anything that might bring on symptoms. They were coming on their own in unpredictable fashion. I wasn't going to do anything to provoke them. Go to bed early. Wake up early. Eat well. I had to do everything I could to be safe from the symptoms.

I didn't plan to marry or have kids. I was managing some trips and exercising and working my job and dealing with my illness in my own way. I was able to mountain bike and snow ski every year in Utah and Colorado and the Black Hills. I also took week-long rafting trips in Utah and Wyoming and Colorado. Sometimes I felt great during the trips, other times like hell. Either way, I needed to go. One foot in front of the other. I wouldn't allow myself to give in.

The illness never went away, but it never stayed permanently, either. After a week of being sick, I would think this was it, there was no way out and my life was ruined. Then it would just turn around and I would feel good again, as if a fog lifted. It was one of the best feelings to magically have good health restored.

The converse was true as well. When I would have a good health stretch, the rug would be pulled out from under my feet. One minute I was healthy and the next I could become sick, suddenly and debilitatingly. It was an intermittent, frustrating cycle.

Chapter 20

St. Joseph's Indian School

In the meantime, I was mostly enjoying my work at St. Joe's. I was raised in South Dakota, but I was taught nothing about the state's history with its Indigenous people and knew nothing about the Native children when I went to work with them. I had no lofty ideals of going to the school to try to "save" kids. I have met some who come to the school for that reason and I find it insulting. It generally doesn't end well for either the kids or for the person with the patriarchal, patronizing approach.

I didn't really consider the backgrounds of the children that much before taking the job, which I suppose was naive and insulting in its own way. I was 25 when I arrived there; I knew I needed employment and the position I was offered matched my field of study.

As initiation, and possibly to challenge my lack of awareness, I was given a good run for my money by the kids the first couple of years. The students forced me to earn their trust and to build relationships with them.

Looking back, I'm proud of them for putting me through my paces. I was sick, which made my occupational and cultural growing pains even more difficult, but I don't want the kids at the school to trust just anyone.

On my first day of work in July of 1994, it was the heart of summer, so there were no kids on campus. My boss decided to send me traveling by myself to one of the local reservations, Lower Brule, which is about 40 miles away from Chamberlain.

She had tasked me with securing signatures from a fifth grade female student's parent on a yearly school consent form that hadn't been signed the previous spring. It would be necessary when the school year began again in the fall. The young girl would be one of the kids on my caseload.

The parent had filled out almost the entire consent form, but had forgotten to sign a couple of items. It was my job to make sure everything was signed so that his daughter could attend our school.

In Lower Brule, I found the small home of "Bull," the person I was looking for. As I stepped out of my school car with what looked like government license plates and approached his house, he walked out of the house and met me on the sidewalk. I greeted him, told him who I was, and politely asked him to sign the consent form. Bull took off his shirt and said "let's go, right here."

It was my first visit to the reservation with my new job, by myself, and I was being threatened with physical violence. No problem, I certainly wasn't going to fight him. I made it to age 25 without ever taking or throwing a punch and I despised pain.

I turned around and got in the car and drove back to the school. I let my boss know that Bull had tried to fight me. A couple of the older guys, the veterans, told me that Bull had come to the school once before and stood on the front lawn, yelling at the windows and threatening to fight them.

That seemed like poor timing to let me know about the legend of "Fighting Bull Johnson." So there was precedent for his ass-kicking behavior – information I could have used yesterday. Apparently, I was the sacrificial lamb sent to get the signature of somebody they knew was going to be problematic.

I don't think anyone was trying to intentionally haze me, but it was one of those experiences that I guess I needed to go through to gain understanding. It was a quick, though potentially painful, way to learn. So were some of the interactions with kids during the first year or two, when they would make fun of me or avoid me.

Most of the students were reasonably kind to me, but there were some that just weren't going to warm up immediately. They seemed determined to make me even more aware that I was the new guy and this was their school.

They were right. They wanted to make sure I knew I was out of my element, which I was, and I didn't always realize it. I didn't have a right to come into their school and tell them what to do.

I learned a lot about my attitude towards the kids, their families, and their culture and history that first year. I didn't intentionally walk in with a patriarchal or colonial attitude, but their mindsets and their history of traumatization had prepared them for that, and that was what mattered.

If I was going to serve them and their families, I needed to be acutely aware of my approach. The kids and their families were going to be the ones to teach me. It was up to me to listen.

As with most things in my life, it took me a while to get it. This was partly due to the fact that I was young, partly because I was going through an illness that was trying to extinguish my young adulthood, and partly because I was focused on my social anxiety much of the time.

But, once I figured out that I needed to humble myself, I was at least on the right path.

Chapter 21

Inípi

When I first came to St. Joe's, there was a sizable number of young adult staff there, twenty-somethings from all over the country. It had been one of the draws for me to be there. But then, the illness set in and there was no chance of me interacting with these people in any way, my age or not.

I didn't leave my house. I would hear tales of them going to the bar or gathering for parties, smoking weed and dancing in the rain up at the rest area after their shifts ended. It was not all debauchery and blowing off steam, though. There was a small group who would attend inípi, or sweat lodge, ceremonies from time to time and they always invited me to come with them.

I don't remember who was coming to the campus to be the leader for the sweats or to pour water for them, possibly an elder from the Crow Creek Bad Nation area. I didn't know and it didn't matter– I knew I wouldn't even consider going in. I was afraid I would panic and freak out and it would be a bad experience for everyone.

I didn't know much about inípi, but I knew they were dark and enclosed. Dark enclosed spaces didn't seem like any kind of a way for me to heal from my Chronic Fatigue Syndrome. They seemed like a splendid way to make it worse or to make me lose my mind. So, it would be 10 years of refused invitations before I would actually go into the sweat lodge.

In 2004, my boss told the clinical services staff that we would all be involved in training for the ceremony. An elder would come in to conduct the training and we would all participate in the ceremony as a department after.

Obviously, I had grave reservations about this, as well as sleepless nights worrying about it. It gave me a reason to think about leaving the job, actually. I didn't think I could survive the lodge and didn't want anyone, especially my co-workers, to witness me having that kind of anxiety or panic attack. I couldn't think of anything less dignified than having my long-anticipated psychotic break with witnesses.

The wheels were in motion, though, and we began our training with Francis Whitebird from Pierre. He was a Rosebud Lakota man who worked in state government after receiving an advanced degree from Harvard and serving the United States Army in the Vietnam war.

Francis spoke the Lakota language and had always been involved in ceremonies.

He came to the school and began with our group of counselors, giving instruction as to what we might expect in an inípi ceremony, sharing the purpose of the sacred ceremony and offering his general wisdom to us. The idea, I think, was that our group of counselors would guinea pig the departmental sweats and then the rest of our staff at the school would participate, making us, collectively as school staff, more culturally aware and involved.

In the end, only part of our counseling group ended up taking part in the inípi on Native American Day 2005. No other departments that I am aware of received the instruction and those in my group who were serious about not going into the sweat were able to avoid it.

As for me, ever the faithful servant, I wound up in the lodge on that fall day. It was a mixed sweat, meaning that men and women would go into the lodge together to pray and sing. Francis poured water that day and there were eight or 10 of us altogether. As predicted, I had a panic attack, because that's still what I would often do at that point. On a positive note, I did not have a psychotic break and the panic attack was self-limited. It ended, as all panic attacks have for time immemorial.

I remember sitting in the dark knowing that I would have to pray out loud and knowing that others would hear my voice trembling. Others would know that I was an incompetent failure because I was not strong enough to speak in front of people and might not be able to withstand the heat and enclosed space of the ceremony.

Despite all I had learned, I was still measuring my worth in life based on whether or not I could project complete calm and control. I was definitely in need of further understanding.

There was also special significance that day because my future wife was in the lodge during that mixed sweat. Of course, neither of us knew that she would be my wife someday, although I think we were both secretly hoping something might happen between us. LaRayne had been in sweat a couple of times before and I certainly didn't want to embarrass myself in front of her.
We weren't yet dating at that point and hadn't even really shown our affection for one another.

She was the Native American studies teacher at the school and had been for three years. She played a big part in getting the inípi prepared that day. Francis was one of her mentors and elders in learning Lakota culture, language and ceremony.

LaRayne's first time in ceremony led to a transformation for her. She remembers coming out of the lodge and seeing the world as brand new, knowing instinctively that all things were connected.

Earlier that year, LaRayne's husband since 1990, Trevis Willard, had been experiencing extremely painful headaches; they went to the hospital and discovered he had a tumor the size of a grapefruit on his brain. He was immediately rushed to Sioux Falls for a biopsy. Due to complications from the biopsy, he was placed in a medically induced coma the next week at the Mayo Clinic. He was taken off of life support with LaRayne's permission on Friday, January 29, 2005.

He was buried on LaRayne's Groundhog's Day birthday that year, February 2nd. LaRayne was left a widow with three teenage girls to raise without their father.

I knew the family because LaRayne had been working at St. Joe's since 2002. We had become work acquaintances and I thought she was one of the kindest people I had ever met. Also, she was very pretty. I was glad she was happily married with children, though, otherwise I would have suffered a panic attack worrying about how I would summon courage to ask her on a date.

In 2003, I bought a house along the river from Trevis and LaRayne, who were selling because the house had grown too small for their expanding family. I had been a renter up to that point. When I moved to Chamberlain in 1994, I lived in a beat up rental house across from the National Guard armory for the first year.

In the spring of 1995, I received insider information at St. Joe's that a young houseparent couple and their two kids were moving out of a rental house along the river. Josephine Raish was their neighbor. She owned the rental that would soon be vacant. She was elderly and I knew that she likely knew both of my grandmothers.

In an act of unusual boldness for me, I parked Sunshine Daydream in front of her house, knocked on her door and told her who I was. I mentioned that I was Marie Woster's grandson – she lit up and shared that she had played in a social band back in the day with my grandma Marie. They were a jug band of sorts, with my grandma as the anchor since she played an actual instrument.

Grandma Marie was a self-taught piano player. The word is that she jumped on a piano when she was little and was immediately able to play. She was at home with ragtime numbers and Liberace songs. She liked happy songs that made people, and her, feel good.

Her piano was a focal point for us grandkids when we went to visit her while growing up. We would often gather around the piano and sing Christmas carols. Her jug band with Josephine and others was named the Teabags, and some of the other ladies played washboards and mops and buckets and kazoos and anything else that might make noise that transformed into rhythm or melody.

I have since heard that the ladies would also meet under the pretense of being a weight loss group, but would actually bring all sorts of food and play their instruments and dance around in their stockings to music. Small wonder that I wanted to be a rock star my entire life.

Josephine liked the idea of having me as a neighbor, but I didn't realize that she was not yet aware that the young couple planned to move. She was shocked at the news. I felt bad that I unintentionally betrayed the couple's confidence.

No matter, though. A few weeks later, everything fell into place and I took over a river home rental for $290 a month, a staggeringly small amount of money for a full house with two bedrooms with a view of the Missouri River with nightly sunsets over the western bluffs. I didn't use much of the house, but it suited my needs and would for the next eight years.

I was pretty sure there were two types of people in the world, owners and renters. I was also pretty sure that I was a renter. Owning something didn't feel quite right to me, although I did own a pickup truck. Real estate was not my thing.

I was never destined to make money. I only earned money in order to be able to afford the occasional biking, rafting or ski trip. I didn't even really have enough money to own a home or to go into debt with a mortgage.

LaRayne can be pretty persuasive, though, and in 2003 she was trying to convince me that her family's home would be perfect for me to buy – I shouldn't continue to throw my money away on a rental. Instead, I should begin to accrue equity in the home she was attempting to sell me.

I have a very commonsensical, financially prudent uncle whom I spoke with during spring break in Moab between mountain bike rides and over dinner. He agreed with LaRayne, suggesting that it only made sense to take the plunge. I should put my rental money into a house of my own so I could have something to show for it besides a hole in the air.

When I returned from Moab, I took the first steps towards buying the house. As with my rental, it was way too much house for me when I moved in, but I fell in love with it and loved having something more permanent for myself. Did I mention it was on the river?

I was single and I was happy. LaRayne was able to afford a log cabin across the river in Oacoma that had more bathrooms and bedrooms for her three growing girls, so she was happy, too.

Of course, not even two years later tragedy struck and Trevis died suddenly at 38 years of age. LaRayne turned 36 on the day of his funeral and became a young widow with three suddenly fatherless children. They were devastated.

Chapter 22

They Love Each Other

I always had eyes for LaRayne, but wouldn't have dreamed of encroaching upon the life of her three daughters. They lost their father and loved him very much. They did not need a replacement. I could fantasize about a relationship with her, but I knew everything about it was impractical, probably impossible. I was committed to suffering alone with my illness and the last thing she and the girls needed, in my estimation, was a replacement husband and father. LaRayne and I all had multiple and unequivocal reasons for not pursuing a relationship together.

But, as time passed into late 2005, we would find opportunities to spend a little time together. I would see her out on the river while I was boating with my family and she with her kids. We would make trips to cross country meets together, where she had a daughter running and a student of mine competed. We teamed up with Schoeny to compete in a triathlon in the summer.

In early October 2005, we had the Native American day inípi at the school. To my relief, I survived and didn't have a panic attack that debilitated me (to be clear, I did have a panic attack, I was just able to push through it). The lodge was brutally hot that day, but it was clear that something special was happening spiritually inside the lodge for myself and the others. We shared prayers and sang songs. With the door closed and in the complete dark, it becomes easier to share deep, powerful emotions and prayer. The connection between all of us was strong.

As nervous as I had been, I lost all my reservations about simply surviving inípi when the time came. The ceremony resonated with me in a way that church never completely did. The intensity of the heat and the connection with the natural world were what I had been looking for. Inhibitions are forgotten in the lodge with the heat, darkness, songs, and prayer. I was hooked and grateful for the acceptance of those who invited me.

Since that day, I have taken part in hundreds of inípi ceremonies. Things become real between participants. Pretense is dropped and people are honest with each other, and themselves. This shedding of the ego is exactly what I was looking for and I learn something new each time I attend.

On the night before the state cross country meet two weeks later, LaRayne and I, along with her daughter Jordan, went out to eat before dropping Jordan off for a football game. LaRayne and I decided to hang out a little while the game was going on and LaRayne agreed to come to my house.

Mine was the house she had raised her girls in and had lived with her husband for so many years. I asked her if she had any misgivings and wanted to go somewhere else because of the history of the place. In true LaRayne fashion, she did not.

She does not tend to dwell on the past and is generally a forward thinker. While someone else might lose themselves in sorrow and grief and let things fall apart, that was just not her manner. She does not typically suffer from angst.

So, we found ourselves in the living room. I sat at one end of the couch, veritably miles away from her on the other end. It seemed as if the couch was twice as big as it really measured.

Some things never change, particularly my inability to assert myself with a woman. Luckily, LaRayne took pity on me and realized the predicament I was in as a basket case. She was forward enough to ask me what we were doing with our relationship.

I stuttered and stammered and she finally let me off the hook and said she thought that we should be pursuing something a little deeper. I was able to tell her that I would like that, but I wanted to make sure that the girls were OK with it. If they weren't, even a little bit, we wouldn't push this any further.

She assured me that they were her girls and she understood them. She would help them through it and that everything would be fine. Of course, LaRayne was right and her Jedi mind tricks ensured things worked out for us.

The girls have all said they wanted to make life miserable for me, but were unable to for a couple reasons. For one, I didn't really do anything that was threatening to their way of life and because I was just too goofy and non-threatening to treat badly. Also, because they wanted to please their mom and they saw that she was happy with me.

I need to be very clear that, had it been left to me, I would still be sitting in my old house in Chamberlain, daring to phone every once in a while, making up excuses as to why we should drive together to a cross country meet. Fortunately, LaRayne had the sense that first night (probably before that night) to know we needed to be together, likely for all time. She also knew that we needed to have a child of our own together.

I protested some because of my illness and my plans to never have a wife or children. Getting together with her would uproot all those impediments to my future plans. I'd been nursing these delusions since getting sick and they were about to be gone in one fell swoop. I would have a girlfriend, then a wife, then three daughters...an instant family with the potential for one on the way.

I went to bed that night before the state cross country meet in 2005 and didn't sleep. I knew what a mess I had been off and on for 11 years. I wasn't capable of expressing to her just how bad things could be for me at times. When I tried, she just assured me that she could handle it, and so could her girls. I wasn't sure I believed her, but I desperately wanted to because I knew that I was already in love with her.

She was certain about a future with me and I loved her. I now knew that the only things holding us back were my illness, crippling social anxiety, and a fear of committing to something that could ruin both of our lives, along with the lives of her three children.

No big deal, right?

Well, it was a big deal. I knew if I committed to her and the girls it couldn't just be to date for a while. For me, I needed to commit forever or not at all. I tossed and turned all night and experienced all of my Chronic

Fatigue symptoms and knew that her proposal of a deeper relationship had kicked a relapse back into action. Well, if I was relapsing, she would see me fall apart the next day and she would rescind her interest in me.

It turns out that I awoke the next morning and had magically made the decision that I would commit for the rest of my life. I can't explain much farther than that. I was in love and needed to be all-in. And I was.

Whatever spell she put on me, it was a good one. It was truly the easiest thing I have ever done. All of the terrible things I'd imagined for twelve years disappeared and I couldn't have been happier. In fact, she didn't really have to deal with my sickness, either, because it seemed to disappear almost immediately. I was as healthy as I had been since 1993. Whether I wanted to admit it or not, it was because of her and my new family.

I was astonished. Suddenly, by late 2005, at just shy of 37 years of age, my life seemed to be back on track. The past 11 years of my life had been clouded by a mystery illness that set up residence in my body, brain, and spirit, beating me down. I had been scared, anxious and unwell. But now, I was with my dream girl and she thought that literally everything I did was great, which was a brand new experience for me.

Her girls accepted me, at least at face value, as a valued member of their family. They understood my worth to their mother's happiness in the wake of losing her first husband. They must have had concerns, but they didn't air them to me and they treated me with respect and care.

I went to all of their many activities – ball games, concerts, everything. My schedule outside of work had always been busy with traveling, playing in a band, listening to music, reading books, golfing with my friend Chris and his boys (I didn't really like golf, but it was a good excuse to hang with my brother Chris), and biking. But, when I got with LaRayne, my schedule exploded. It probably didn't leave me any time to be sick.

We dated for a few months and in March 2006, she insisted that I move into her log cabin home with the four of them. Again, if she hadn't insisted, I would likely still be a bachelor in my own home in Chamberlain. When I moved in with her, we made the decision to sell my old house, the one that used to belong to her and her family.

We sold it on our own fairly quickly and closed the chapter of our lives at that residence forever.

Since moving to Chamberlain 11 years earlier, I'd spend a lot of time with my grandmother Lorene. Shortly after I moved in with LaRayne, I went to my cherished grandmother and asked for her mother's ring. Ada Leiferman's wedding ring was 100 years old and I was going to use it to propose to LaRayne.

I actually asked my mom about Great Grandma Ada's ring first. I was not surprised at mom's reaction. She was overjoyed. She loved LaRayne and her girls from the minute she met them and was thrilled that we had found each other. She wanted me to have the ring.

So, I approached the back door of my grandma's home one evening just as I had so many times in the past. As one might guess, I was in a state of panic about asking her, even though I knew she would say yes. She loved LaRayne and she would love the thought of a family heirloom being handed down and staying in the family.

My anxiety reared its ugly head, though, and a completely reasonable situation became irrational in my mind once again.

I knocked on the door and, looking through the glass of her back door, I watched her come from the kitchen and approach the landing that would lead down the steps to where I stood expectantly outside the back door. On her way, she yelled one of her usual greetings to me to "get in this house, Scotchman," which I did. I stood at the bottom of the stairs with her slight frame towering over me on the upper landing. I managed to blurt out something about asking LaRayne to marry me and wondering if I could have her mom's ring from 1906 to use as the wedding ring.

There was a long pause...and then she iced me. She told me she would think about it and let me know. I must have mumbled something more and left the house wondering how, of all the possible outcomes I had pondered, that one had not occurred to me.

Actually, there had only been one possible outcome that had occurred to me–elation and a woman on the verge of 90 sprinting up her stairs. She would collect the ring from its treasured spot where she had kept it for safekeeping, waiting for this exact moment.

I would have been disappointed by her reaction, but, as I said, I was in love. It would have taken quite a bit to knock me down from my cloud.

Of course, she called the next day to say that she was thrilled and that I could, naturally, have the ring. She just needed to check with my mom to make sure because it was technically hers. Whatever the case, asking LaRayne to marry me was going to be a breeze after that affair.

I told LaRayne, likely on that night in late October 2005 when we were struggling to define and declare our intentions to each other, that I had no need to be married. I was content having a relationship with her in whatever capacity suited us both best.

She told me that the girls, young as they were, would want their mom to be married and not just living with a guy or dating him forever, in sickness or in health. The girls were devout Catholic Christians and didn't believe in a man and woman living together when they were not married.

LaRayne did not share the same concerns as the girls but, in order to put their desires first (which is what we both wanted) we decided we should get married. Marriage had always made me nervous. I had been to many weddings and I mostly paid attention to the things that a groom would do that would cause me anxiety.

Grooms walk up the aisle, in clothes they would never normally wear, while a crowd of people stare at them and judges how well they are getting on. I didn't want anyone to know that I wasn't holding up and that I was actually having a panic attack. It gets worse, though. The groom then has to stand in front of all those people and actually speak, which I couldn't do in that situation, and declare his love to his bride in front of everyone they know.

I had always known that the prospect of anxiety turning the best day of my life into the worst was a real thing. It was going to either keep me from getting married or expose my anxiety to everyone whose opinion mattered to me.

Committing to LaRayne on that October evening in 2005 was an all-or-nothing proposition for me. I hadn't dated in 12 years and I certainly didn't do one-night stands. I hadn't touched a woman in that period of time. I was not interested in leading someone else on, or leading myself on, unless I meant it.

This time, with LaRayne, I meant it. Because I meant it, I had to be completely honest with her about a few parameters for me.

I needed her to know how bad the chronic fatigue was for me at times. I wanted to let her know how fragile I could be and how that would be a burden for her. She didn't care and said that she would support me no matter what. She truly was not concerned. She obviously had never experienced anxiety before and typically lives with the belief that everything will be fine, which is nothing short of ludicrous, ridiculous and unimaginable to an anxiety-riddled person.

Secondly, I needed her to know that I would get married, but that it couldn't be in a church. Organized religion just didn't mean a great deal to either of us for numerous reasons and was a deal-breaker for me. She agreed.

Third, I let her know that there would be no diamonds. I strongly believed that diamonds are a poor symbol and representation of someone's love. I felt that my grandma's 100-year-old ring was a better reflection. Check. She agreed.

Finally, I had to make her promise that I wouldn't have to say anything during the service and that there would be as few people as possible there. She again agreed. I didn't explain to her that it was due to social anxiety because I still didn't want to fully expose her to that part of myself.

On March 15th, 2006, during spring break from the school, we drove to Pierre to have lunch with my parents and I took LaRayne to a beach on the west side of Lake Oahe, just above the dam. My family had been going there, especially with two other families, since I was a kid.

My mom had been a young nurse in Pierre and she met two other nurses at her job. The three would take their young kids to the beaches on their days off. Eventually, they brought their husbands along. With the husbands came boats and it turned into water skiing and camping weekends up and down the Missouri River and Lake Oahe from Memorial Day to Labor Day every year.

One of the beaches above the dam was home to our families frequently, especially as we got older, and it came to be known as “Nancy’s beach,” after my mom. There, I proposed to LaRayne. It was late morning on Phil Lesh’s birthday (Grateful Dead bass player) and the Ides of March, when Caesar was assassinated by his good chum Brutus.

Surprisingly, I had never felt more composed and confident, far more so than when I asked Grandma Lorene for the ring. I asked without hesitation and LaRayne accepted without hesitation. I presented her with a ring that had been around for a century; a family heirloom. She treasures it.

Chapter 23

Type 1 Diabetes

Two of LaRayne's girls, Jordan and Frankie, were diagnosed with type 1 diabetes when they were young. I can't stress strongly enough the dangers of living with type 1 diabetes; the constant monitoring and correction of blood sugar levels is literally a matter of life and death.

It's a manageable illness, but it takes ongoing surveillance and, even then, things can go wrong. They did just that for Jordan during the summer after her eighth-grade year in 2006 – one month before our wedding.

She did not feel well for a couple of days, but her insulin pump and monitors showed that her diabetes was well-controlled. As she became increasingly more ill over those days that seemed like years, the situation finally came to a head. Her mom went to work early one morning so she could miss part of the work day in order to take Jordan to a doctor's appointment.

I was preparing to leave for work early that morning as well. I went downstairs and saw Jordan walking across the room to use the bathroom, only wearing a T-shirt.

I knew at that point that Jordan was completely unaware of her surroundings. I helped her get dressed and called LaRayne to meet us at the emergency room. I put Jordan in the car and rushed to the hospital. She was so disoriented that, by the time we arrived at the hospital, she had pressed her feet against the dashboard and her back against the car seat so that I couldn't get her out of the vehicle.

Once we were finally able to remove her and take the steps to get her into a room, her reading for blood sugar was so high that it was no longer registering as a number.

Chamberlain hospital staff thought at that point it was close to 900, which is well within the diabetic coma range. They needed to put her on an IV, which went into her neck because they weren't able to locate any of her veins due to her condition. Quick thinking by her nurse Kala Shepherd likely saved her life.

Kala was able to contact the doctor, who was working at the outreach clinic that day in LaRayne's hometown of Kennebec – 40 miles away. The two of them determined that Jordan needed to be moved to Sioux Falls and the larger Sanford hospital as quickly as possible. Her blood sugar level needed to be brought down very slowly to avoid damage to her brain and body.

Decreasing a blood sugar level that high too rapidly, we were told, can cause a whole host of problems–organ failure, brain damage and even death. Jordan was intubated and loaded into an airplane. She and her mom were flown 140 miles to Sioux Falls that afternoon. I sped home, packed up a few clothes for the three of us and raced to follow. It certainly felt like the truck and I made the two-hour drive at speeds very close to air travel.

I arrived at the hospital shortly after LaRayne and Jordan. The doctor greeted us and reiterated that they were going to have to bring her blood sugar down as slowly as possible. It was, indeed, a matter of life and death. We wouldn't know for at least 24 hours if she was even going to live, let alone without lasting effects, possibly brain damage. LaRayne and I stayed at the hospital, keeping vigil at her bedside.

At the end of approximately 24 agonizing hours, Jordan came back to us and we knew, miraculously, that she would be fine. In the end, we learned that her equipment malfunctioned – it was reflecting a good reading when, in fact, her blood sugar was rising to dangerous and eventually life-threatening levels. It drove home the reality that Type 1 diabetes is deadly if not managed correctly every day.

While all this was happening, another very important event was about to take place.

It is traditional in LaRayne's Lakota culture to plan and prepare a memorial after a year of grieving for the loss of a loved one. LaRayne had scheduled a memorial and celebration of life for Trevis more than a year after his death, instead choosing to have it on his birthday, June 11th. The event would be held at the golf course where he excelled and where he loved to spend time, both with his friends and family, and with his wife and couples' golf partner, LaRayne. Fittingly, it also included a golf tournament.

A memorial includes a giveaway, in which gifts are given to those present. It involves providing a meal for those gathered and, most importantly, requires the mental and emotional preparation necessary to meet with loved ones to remember a life, share laughter and memories, and to cry, grieving the loss all over again.

I had been engaged to LaRayne for two months at that point and we were to be wed in one. But, make no mistake, she made all the preparations necessary - gifts, meal and psyche. In true LaRayne fashion, she made a commitment for the ceremony, and, in both

LaRayne's and the native way, you do not break your commitment.

LaRayne, Jordan and I were discharged from the hospital in Sioux Falls on the morning of June 11th. We drove to Chamberlain, gathered what we needed for the memorial and left for the golf course.

We gathered with friends and family as planned and LaRayne gave away star quilts and other gifts to Trevis' loved ones.

Some of the gifts had been his belongings and some were bought or made with the recipient in mind. She even gave away a brand new puppy to his brother-in-law. It is a powerful way to remember your loved one and it marked the ceremonial end to the symbolic first year of LaRayne's grieving for her late husband.

Chapter 24

Weddings

When LaRayne and I were wed in July 2006, we had two days of ceremony. The first day, we drove to the old Woster farm south of Medicine Butte near Reliance, about 15 miles from the log cabin in Oacoma where we were living at the time. This farm is where my father grew up. His dad and uncle shared the Woster Brothers' brand, raising a modest amount of cattle and farming the land.

My ancestry has always been important to me and this has always been a special place. LaRayne agreed to marry me, with only the three girls present as witnesses, on the front stoop of the old farmhouse, though the structure was no longer standing.

My dad's cousin, Ronald "Red" McManus, was the mayor of Reliance at that time. He agreed to meet us there – a place that was meaningful to him as well – to legalize our marriage on the virtual front step with his powers as Justice of the Peace. It was a beautiful ceremony on a piece of land with a strong spiritual attachment for my Woster and McManus sides of the family. Now, it's fortified with the commitments to my new family, LaRayne and the girls.

After the ceremony, we left the old farm and drove through the nearby Lower Brule reservation to get to Pierre. There, we took part in an inípi ceremony at a friend's lodge just 10 miles or so east of Pierre – my old stomping grounds. We planned to hold a ceremony with our family members in the lodge. Our good friend Schoeny was going to pour water and lead both the women's and men's ceremony.

The women, along with Schoeny, went into the ceremony at two or three o'clock, as the thermostat outside the lodge topped out at 110 degrees. It was the first time in an inípi ceremony for the girls, and for my mother and sister. They each had their reservations about the ceremony, but they all wanted to participate and support LaRayne and me on our special day.

One by one, though, they came out from the lodge appearing defeated at best and, in some cases, downright incapacitated. They all went back to town to enjoy a shower and air conditioning. Schoeny remained in the lodge with LaRayne and Kristi, her brother Keith's wife. They seemed to have no problem withstanding the heat. They were able to focus on their prayer, sharing with the creator and with the people who needed help in this world.

Once the women's ceremony was over, it was time for the men to crawl in. My father, my brother-in-law and my brother were a bit nervous for their first sweat ceremony. After all, they had just witnessed the ladies exiting one by one in varying states of distress.

As the men ended our first round, everyone was doing well, apart from Schoeny. He tipped over as a result of the prolonged heat of the two sweats. Out of necessity, some of the ceremony was completed with the flaps on the lodge open so Schoeny could withstand his second inípi in a row. Even with the flaps open, we were still letting in the 110-degree summer heat.

The legal and inípi ceremonies complete, we all went into Pierre to share a meal at my parents' house. On our second wedding day, everyone woke in the morning and we drove up to Lake Oahe and "Nancy's beach" for the Lakota ceremony.

We had a friend from St. Joe's sew traditional ribbon shirts and a skirt for LaRayne. We stood barefoot on a bison robe, surrounded by our close family, while Schoeny blessed us with his sacred pipe. He sang a Lakota song in our honor and our families blessed us with their prayers.

Afterwards, we went back to Pierre to my parents' house where LaRayne and I had a giveaway, which is traditional in the Lakota culture. In the preceding months, we made – in some cases, bought – gifts for our loved ones.

I put fringe on the shawls LaRayne had sewn for our nieces, Schoeny made hand drums from elk and bison hide for my brothers. We had friends make star quilts for our parents and for Schoeny.

After our post-wedding meal, which LaRayne and I cooked as a gift to those who came, we passed the gifts to each of them one by one and talked about what they meant to us. It was heartfelt and moving. I would not have dreamed of doing this without LaRayne's influence and, obviously, without the influence of the Lakota culture. The giveaway is a powerful display of selflessness for Native American people.

The next day, Schoeny departed for his sundance near Cheyenne Crossing in the Black Hills of western South Dakota. Schoeny had been dancing at sundances even before he returned from Alaska to live in South Dakota in 2004. In Alaska, he met a Lakota mentor who recognized his strong heart and encouraged him to join a sundance near Eagle Butte, South Dakota, on the Cheyenne River reservation.

Schoeny came to work at St. Joseph's in Chamberlain when he returned permanently from Alaska. At St. Joe's, he met a man named John Beheler who invited him to participate in a sundance in the Black Hills.

Schoeny left the day after our wedding for the week-long ceremony where he would fast and pray and dance in the sun until the next Sunday, one week. Through the cultural experiences of her adult life, LaRayne was familiar with the sundance and had been to them before. I, however, had little understanding of what would transpire.

During the week after our wedding, we woke early one morning and made the four-hour drive to the Black Hills sundance grounds. My younger brother Andy joined us; we would spend the day watching Schoeny and John dance.

At some point that day, John and Schoeny guided LaRayne and me into the center of the sundance circle. They led us to the sacred grandfather tree to have the leader (who was John's adoptive father, Chuck Ross), bless our marriage. It was an unbelievably powerful experience to be in the center of that hóčhokaŋ wakȟáŋ (sacred circle) and to have our marriage blessed in such a spiritually meaningful manner.

Following our wedding and the blessing in the summer of 2006, we lived in the log cabin in Oacoma. LaRayne and I experienced wedded bliss while the teenagers were happily involved in school activities and focused on classic teen pastimes such as athletics and young love.

During this time, and well before this time, LaRayne talked about having another child with me. As if the idea of marriage and raising three stepdaughters wasn't daunting enough, she now wanted to change my life further by having us bring new life into this world.

She is persuasive, though, and I knew early on that we were going to have a child together. LaRayne was 38 at the time and we both knew that we wouldn't have much time left to make that choice. We came to a mutual decision to wait a brief time while we settled into our new routine, and then began to prepare for another life.

Chapter 25

Omens

Approaching Easter in 2007, LaRayne became pregnant. Our family celebrated the idea of bringing a new sibling on board. The girls were thrilled with the idea and we excitedly planned for a new baby.

A month or so into the pregnancy, on a Sunday afternoon, LaRayne began experiencing cramping and blood spotting. When it didn't get any better that evening, she called the emergency room in Chamberlain and they urged her to remain calm and see how her symptoms progressed through the rest of the evening and overnight.

We retired to bed after praying together that our little baby would be born healthy in seven or eight months. I remember lying awake in bed with the windows open, unable to sleep. Through the night I would hear an owl outside the window.

I did not say anything to LaRayne about it during the night, but the next morning she let me know that she had heard an owl outside the window as well. She also didn't sleep through the night.

Sometime mid- to late-morning, LaRayne had a miscarriage. In the Native culture, the appearance of an owl can be interpreted as a bad omen, a premonition that death or something harmful could be imminent. I wasn't aware at the time, but one of LaRayne's aunts, Winifred Andrews, heard an owl the night Trevis died. In the Lakota way of life, these signs from nature are not regarded as simple superstitions. These are viewed as true omens and reminders to hold mother earth close and to walk a good red road in this life.

We have spoken with spiritual leaders about the situation, and we're told that an owl doesn't necessarily indicate a bad omen. Sometimes its presence can be a reminder to pray and to remain focused on good.

In Native American culture, literally everything is tied to the natural world. Our elders taught us these things and we hold on to them tightly.

Our family was devastated by the loss of this baby, whom we ended up calling Spirit, or sacred being. LaRayne went to the hospital that day and was able to bring home a small box with the tissue of the baby that had passed from her. We traveled to Pierre, to Nancy's Beach and our sacred wedding spot, where we built a small fire. There, we buried the remains of our child, returning the little one to mother earth.

The ground there will forever remain sacred to the two of us for so many reasons.

Because the cycle of life waits for no one and because LaRayne has a well-honed righting instinct, she was soon pregnant again. We decided early on that we would name our child Sage, whether boy or girl.

We were certain that we would have a boy this time. LaRayne had given birth to three girls at this point and her brother Keith had three girls and was on his way to adding two more. Her brothers Russell and Craig had girls. The only family member who didn't have girls was her brother Lenny, who had three boys.

Around the time that LaRayne was discovering she was pregnant for the second time with someone who would be called Sage, we were lamenting the fact that we didn't keep my house on River Street in Chamberlain.

At the time of our wedding, we made the decision to remain in the log cabin in Oacoma and sell the River Street house because their family had moved out of it for several reasons. They needed a larger house–one bathroom wasn't going to suffice for a family of five. All three girls shared a loft bedroom and, as teenagers, needed their own space. The log cabin provided a bedroom for each.

Possibly the most important factor for LaRayne and I choosing the log cabin was that there remained so many memories of their family in the home on River Street. We decided it would be too difficult for the girls and for LaRayne to try to live in a house that was filled with so many associations with their late father and husband. It was a choice that made sense at the time, but we both missed living next to the river.

During a bike ride in the summer of 2007, LaRayne and I discovered that the house two doors down from the River Street house was for sale. It had ample space, with rooms for all of us, and was on the river in the old neighborhood. It was overpriced, but we couldn't help ourselves–bought with our hearts instead of our heads and haven't looked back.

Life was busy at the end of summer 2007. LaRayne was newly pregnant, we were moving and settling into a new home and Jackie, the oldest daughter, was preparing to graduate and move on to college. As always, LaRayne handled these major life changes like she had done it all many times before.

LaRayne handled pregnancy like a natural and guided me through those nine months so that I felt as if I had done it before too. It was remarkable that I didn't feel any anxiety as I prepared to become the father of a baby for the first time, and it was largely due to her calming influence.

By 2008, I had been working with teenagers for 14 years and had been with LaRayne's teens in the same home for the last two years. Up until about age 12, kids were pretty much a mystery to me. It's a testament to the rock that LaRayne is: a typically anxious guy like me felt the calm of a seasoned professional during this period. It is also a testament to the love I was feeling for LaRayne at this time. Things that normally bothered me just didn't because of her.

I was blissfully unaware of how the community, some friends, and even some family members might be viewing our relationship and our new life. I acknowledged that there was still pain for those who lost a close friend, community member, and family member in Trevis. But I was in love and moving at warp speed, unable to give such thoughts much consideration.

I followed my wife's lead and focused on the life we were living at the moment we were living it. We didn't have much time to approach it any other way, and we still don't.

Chapter 26

Sage

By early February 2008, LaRayne had enough of pregnancy and was ready to give birth. We made three trips to the hospital that month, including on our due date of February 20, only to be turned away and told she wasn't ready yet. Finally, on the morning of February 22, LaRayne's water broke and we rushed to the hospital. They sent us home again, but told us that the birth could be imminent and that we should just stay around the house and relax that day.

By late afternoon, LaRayne was experiencing contractions and had enough of relaxing. I didn't know just how over it she was until I saw her walk by the window of the house, suitcase in hand. She was on her way to the hospital. I chased after her, loaded her into the truck and we sped up the hill yet again. Upon arrival at the emergency room parking lot, she was wracked with more contractions just outside the door of the emergency room.

I watched helplessly as she hugged a concrete pole and squatted down in the ambulance bay, seemingly on the verge of dropping her newborn on the asphalt beneath her. She later joked that this was the way many of her ancestors ended up giving birth, hugging a tree, and she thought it might just happen right there.

Indeed, it did not. At 7:46 PM, from a hospital room, she gave birth to Sage Marie Woster – a baby girl, as we should have expected all along.

We immediately got right down to the business of loving this new life, Sage, and we viewed her as her name might suggest – as medicine. She was good medicine for the entire family.

Sage is a plant that is used for smudging. This rite involves burning the leaves, commonly in an abalone shell, and waving the smoke over your body in order to cleanse yourself before ceremony or during prayer.

Sage was indeed that type of cleansing medicine for us. While she didn't replace a father or fully assuage the grief of losing someone, she arrived at a perfect time for continued healing and lifting of the spirit for our family.

Traditionally, the afterbirth or the placenta of a newborn is buried and returned to earth in a sacred spot. It was here that she was given her first spirit name of Matȟó Wačhípi Wičhíŋčala (Dancing Bear Girl). We gathered close family and had a sacred ceremony in our backyard along the Missouri River. In a circle, we prayed over a string of colored prayer ties filled with tobacco, blessing Sage and planting her placenta in the ground.

We also kept her umbilical cord and put it in a leather satchel that is traditionally worn around the neck. LaRayne beaded a turtle to affix to the top of the leather. The turtle symbolizes long life in the Lakota culture, as well as many others.

Sage was everything I could've hoped for and more in a brand new daughter. After my struggles with anxiety and Chronic Fatigue Syndrome, I had a new lease on life. LaRayne and I embraced the purpose of raising a young child and watching the older three become women, preparing to move on to the next phases in their lives.

In the summer of 2009, LaRayne and I took Sage camping in the Black Hills at Castle Peak and realized that her toilet training was moving in the wrong direction. At 16 months, she was backsliding in her potty-training progress. We also observed that she was constantly thirsty.

LaRayne off-handedly mentioned that we should test her blood sugar with one of her diabetic sisters' meters when we arrived back home. I didn't consider it much because LaRayne and I were not likely genetic carriers of diabetes, so I figured Sage's thirst and delay in toilet habits were unrelated.

When we arrived back in Chamberlain from the camping trip, LaRayne asked Frankie to test Sage with her blood glucose meter. We discovered that Sage's blood sugar was in the 300s. LaRayne immediately began to sob. I either didn't know enough or was in such denial that I didn't believe she had diabetes.

We made an appointment at the hospital and within the next hour the doctor determined that Sage had type 1 diabetes. By 5 p.m., we were in a room at the Sanford Children's Hospital, visiting with doctors and making decisions about how to manage our 16-month-old child's diabetes.

By 6 o'clock, I was plunging her first dose of insulin into her with a needle. It was not something I relished, obviously, but I knew it would be necessary in order to keep her alive every day from then on. It's a powerful, and undesirable, realization to know that I could potentially cost my daughter her life by giving the wrong dose of insulin or by failing to give insulin after a meal or snack.

I had a sharp learning curve for type 1 diabetes. I had to learn quickly in order to make the right decisions for my child, who was unable to take care of herself at that point. Luckily for Sage and me, we had LaRayne. By that point, LaRayne was basically an unregistered diabetic educator due to her years of experience managing the older girls.

By the time I came along and joined the family, both Jordan and Frankie were very independent in managing their condition. They gave themselves injections and made sure their pumps were functioning, taking care of their diabetes in the best way they could.

There was very little for me to do to assist with the diabetic process when I entered their lives. I just watched and marveled at the ease with which they handled it, even though it was far from simple and things could go horribly wrong at any time.

Having that firm knowledge base of diabetes didn’t make Sage’s situation easy for LaRayne. For her, it meant that she now had three type 1 diabetic daughters in the home. We certainly hadn’t heard of that kind of diabetic prevalence in any family then, and we still haven't.

It's highly unusual and probably even more unusual for us because neither LaRayne nor I have any known diabetic carriers in our families. LaRayne worked hard to have our family studied by scientists in order to help isolate a cause or find a cure, but we discovered mostly disinterest and apathy toward our situation.

The Sanford Children's Hospital used our family as a part of their fundraising gala in 2010. A professionally produced video was made of our family, along with families dealing with other childhood diseases. Each of the six or so diseases was given a focus of five minutes in the video and it was presented at their black-tie dinner party at the new Sanford research center that year.

From those childhood illnesses, Denny Sanford and other donors chose type 1 diabetes as Sanford's focus for investing the most money toward discovering a cure. It was a night of hope and excitement. The girls were thrilled to meet such legends as Mike Miller, superstar basketball player from South Dakota, and Olympic swimmer Gary Hall, Jr., who was diagnosed with type 1 diabetes during his gold medal career.

As I write this, it is 15 years since that standout night...but I haven't heard much for updates regarding Sanford's cure for type 1 diabetes. What I have noticed is that they have invested a lot of money in building hospitals and increasing their empire around the globe, and that they continue to build sports arenas for area athletes.

My father, to this day, will not enter a Sanford arena. He sees it as a slight to his three granddaughters who suffer every day with the effects of type 1 diabetes and as a betrayal of the promise made to find the cure.

Chapter 27

Sundance 101

Sage was raised to learn the culture and the history of her Lakota heritage. She was able to live the traditions, attending and participating in powwows. She was crowned Little Miss Chamberlain High School when she was young. She was around our inípi ceremonies and eventually attended sundances and learned the actual living history of her people from very powerful elders. LaRayne and I took justifiable pride in the knowledge that Sage was growing up in this way.

Around the time Sage was born, I began to work with Shawn at St. Joseph's Indian School. He and his grandpa Dino were regularly involved in ceremony, including sundance. When I first met Shawn, he and his grandfather were about to lose their mentor and sundance leader, Elmer. With Elmer's death, Dino learned through visions with the spirits that he would now be the one leading Elmer's sundance.

Dino would be the first to tell you that he is not a medicine man, but is simply an interpreter who quite literally hears and sees visions from the spirits. He began to lead his own sundance shortly after Elmer's death.

In July 2011, Shawn invited LaRayne and me to drive down to the Rosebud reservation to watch Dino's sundance and support the sundancers for a day. As part of my job responsibilities as a counselor at St. Joe's, I am required to travel and to visit my students in the summertime at their homes on the reservations or in the towns where they live around South Dakota. I often pick them up and take them out to eat and we have a chance to hang out and visit. I decided to visit Shawn during the sundance that year and took LaRayne and Sage along with me on a Friday morning.

We had a school vehicle and, as we neared Rosebud, we noticed an intense thunderstorm moving in from the west. We left pavement 15 miles south of Mission, turning west onto a gravel road, and began to drive towards the Sundance grounds. It became apparent that we were heading directly towards this vicious storm. The wind hit the car with tremendous force. The rain poured so heavily that the gravel turned to soup under the car tires almost instantly.

It was 10:00 in the morning, but it seemed like the darkest night had settled in, save for the most brilliant flashes of lightning I have ever seen. The ear-splitting thunder had Sage, then three years old, crying in the back seat.

I decided there was no chance we were going to make it to the grounds and didn't want to take unnecessary risks in someone else's vehicle. I called Shawn; even though he encouraged me to continue driving, I played it safe and turned around.

Just before we reached the pavement again to head north to Mission, the tire on the car exploded. There I was, soaking wet in the thunderstorm lying on the muddy ground, changing the tire as we fled from the storm and the sundance.

Shawn poked fun at me from that day forward and would always say that natives don't run away from something like that – the storm is the thunder beings. They bring blessings and understanding and they are part of his grandpa Dino's sundance medicine bundle altar.

That is all well and good, but I wasn't interested in ruining a company Impala and possibly killing my family for what felt like hubris. We pledged that we would be back next year. I think it's safe to say I received some understanding from the thunder beings that day.

A year later, in July 2012, LaRayne, Sage and I returned to the sundance at the same location. This time we drove our own truck and the weather was blissfully clear. Roughly halfway between Mission, South Dakota and Valentine, Nebraska, we left the heavily-trafficked main highway. The gravel road, which was thankfully dry this year, led us due west for another 10 miles.

In the middle of prairie and farmland, just off of the gravel road on the north side, we saw a cluster of oak and cottonwood trees that blocked the view of the sundance grounds. This seclusion wasn't intentional, I learned later. It's just the lay of the land there. The landowner, a farmer, had agreed to allow the sundance to happen on his property. He farmed the land around the dance grounds and the natural grove of trees made for welcome shade for participants on break and for spectators.

Shawn had invited us to the dance, but we had little connection to anyone else there. I was nervous about stepping on anyone's toes or committing an egregious ceremonial faux pas. And, let's be honest, I was very aware that I was white. How welcome would I be?

All these insecurities and expectations ran through my mind as we pulled up to the people at the front gate who tied a red piece of cloth to our antenna and ushered us through without conversation, which only added to the tension.

It turns out that all of my imaginings about sundance didn't match reality.

The people at the dance had set up a circular arbor that was roughly 100 feet in diameter. The inner ring of the circle was made up of oak trunk "crutches," about 10 feet tall. They are called crutches because they are cut in a Y shape at the top where the first two main branches begin to leave the trunk. The crutches were spaced approximately 10 feet apart and buried in the earth to form a circle. This demarcated the area for dancing.

Ten feet or so outside the first row of oak crutches, another circle of oak crutches were buried in the same manner. In the 10-foot span between each front and back set of crutches, smaller oak trunks rested, suspended horizontally in the Y notches, connecting the inner and outer circles.

This oak trunk setup for the arbor makes a solid base for a thick covering of pine boughs that create a ceiling all the way around the circle. When the dancing takes place on scorching hot summer days, this shade of the boughs provides a cool respite for those in attendance. A well-made arbor is a beautiful sight to behold.

Everything comes from mother earth and from the labor of the dancers and supporters.

For four days leading up to the dance, those involved camp at the grounds and prepare the arbor. Holes are dug, oak trees are cut and transported by flatbed trailer from the dry creek beds to the grounds, as are pine boughs.

Sage plants are cut from the ground where they grow in the surrounding creek beds and fields. Special care is taken to leave enough of the stalk so the plant will flourish there again the next growing season.

There must be enough sage to cover the inside of the dance circle for the dancers to tread upon, for dancers to make crowns, wristlets and anklets to wear, and enough for all the ceremonies that take place before, during, and after the dance. Sweat lodges must be built using willow trees harvested from nearby streams and creeks.

Those are but a few of the examples of the work that is necessary to prepare the grounds and prepare for the dance. Each night, after working in the hot summer sun and heat all day, dancers and other supporters enter the lodge for inípi as part of the four-day purification process.

It is not unusual to go into the lodge at midnight, to sweat in ceremony until two in the morning, go to bed, and then awaken with the sun in a stiflingly hot tent. The sun always comes too early. Regardless, we jump right back into the hard work of using a chainsaw to fell trees and digging holes.

I had no understanding of this on that day in 2012 as we arrived at Dino's dance. I saw everything and it was perfect – it appeared as if it had just always been there. I didn't realize the amount of work that went into what I was witnessing that day.

After the grounds are prepared and the four days of purification are complete, dancers spend four days dancing in a circle in the arbor. They pray for the people, for blessings, for health, help, and goodness.

The day before the dancing starts, a cottonwood tree known as the grandfather is sunk in a massive hole that has been dug in the center of the dance circle. This day is known simply and universally as tree day. In a special ceremony, the tree is cut down with an axe and is not allowed to touch the ground. It is brought to the grounds where it is ceremonially placed in the hole.

From the time the tree goes into mother earth, the dancers are not allowed to talk to anyone but other dancers. At some dances, they are not allowed to eat or drink until completion of the dance in four days. At Dino's dance, many of the dancers are elders, or infirm or simply incapable of fasting for four days, so they are allowed to continue to take their medications, eat and drink to help them withstand the intense heat.

As we pulled into the sundance grounds that day, the dancers were on a break. They were under the shade of the arbor, resting and praying. You could have heard a pin drop as we drove the truck past the arbor while looking for a place to park. It was very uncomfortable for both LaRayne and me since the only person we knew there was Shawn and he was nowhere to be found.

Still at the wheel, I studied the arbor and noticed a man standing right next to the tree in nothing but a handmade skirt that went down to his ankles. He had sage wreaths wrapped with red felt around his head, ankles and wrists.

Shawn quickly found us. He explained that the man in the center of the arbor had already pierced through each side of his chest with eagle bones. These were attached to the two split ends of his rope, which was tied to the tree.

He would remain there with the tree for four days. On the fourth and final day of dancing, the other male dancers would have their chests pierced and be attached to the tree in the same fashion. Finally, they would break away.

My family was receiving a crash course in sundance that was only possible through being there.

It appears that most dances have slight variations in what they believe is the right way. Most of the main themes are congruent between dances, but there are small variations that are noticeable when you have spent enough time around them or talked to enough people who have been to them. Each dance believes they are doing it the correct way. I knew none of this that day. I was simply in awe of what I was witnessing.

LaRayne was more comfortable, as she had been to a few different sundances before and had some notion of what to expect. She knew the proper way to act, the etiquette and even knew some of the songs and was able to dance along from her place under the arbor as a show of support.

For Sage and me, it was a brand-new experience. Sage was four years old now. I spent the day meeting people and realized that I actually knew some people there, including former students and their parents. When each heard that Sage was diabetic, they expressed genuine sympathy for her and our family. Everyone offered to help in any way they could.

I continued to visit with people. One man, Clarence White Horse, and his son (also a former student of mine) DJ, shared that they knew of ceremonies, medicine men and healers across Indian country who could help with Sage's diabetes – even take it away completely.

This was difficult for me to fathom. I had heard stories from old times that told of medicine men taking away ailments and providing cures, but I didn't realize that ceremonies were still occurring. They assured me that they were serious and that the ceremonies were still happening.

I was open-minded enough to believe in the ceremonies and the possibility of healing, but I also realized that I didn't know any healers personally. Something like this wouldn't likely be a fit for Sage, LaRayne, or me.

As I spent the day in that sacred place, watching the dancers and sharing stories with those around me, I thought more and more about how belief, prayer and hope can be life-changing. I came in contact with many people that day who were so life-affirming; they were only at the ceremony to offer and receive the benefit of prayer.

Most of the people I met that day had very little in terms of material possessions. They were asking for nothing but the strength to be able to give what they had to their loved ones and those in need. It was a ceremony of giving and selflessness.

LaRayne and I discussed the conversations we had that day with our new friends about healing ceremonies and medicine men, and about the beauty of the sundance itself. We were captivated. We drove back to Chamberlain that evening as planned, but quickly made plans to return to Rosebud the next morning, on our own time, to be there again and support the dancers.

As I mentioned, there are generally four days of purification and preparation at sundance, followed by four days of dancing. On all four days, dancers begin the day in the arbor at sunrise, dancing with the drum and the singers. They typically continue dancing until sundown or a close approximation.

A round of dancing may last anywhere from 30 minutes to over an hour, depending on the leader and the information he is receiving from spirits while dancing. Dancers have rest periods in between rounds. They sit and pray underneath a dancer-only section of the arbor where they focus their minds on the dance and on those for whom they are praying.

At this dance, as at most dances, the third day was highlighted by the healing round of dancing in the afternoon. This round is particularly special and powerful because supporters or people who have come to watch are allowed to come into the circle to be blessed by the dancers and to drink the medicine for healing.

I have seen many people with many different needs move through the line to be blessed at sundance. Elderly people with age-related infirmities, people suffering from cancer and people with bad backs. But also, people who need a different kind of healing – those with children suffering from alcoholism, people with families damaged by methamphetamine use and people whose children are sick or suicidal.

Dancers are not allowed to have physical contact with the supporters because dancers are believed to be filled with sacred energy. Any touch is made through sage bundles or with eagle fans. Skin-to-skin contact is not allowed.

My first experience with this was at the Black Hills sundance when LaRayne and I were led to the tree by the dancers. We each held onto sage bundles on one end while the dancer who led us to the tree held the bundles on the other end.

On this particular Saturday in Rosebud, LaRayne and I took Sage into the circle and led her past the line of sundancers, stopping briefly in front of and facing each of them, one by one, to have them bless her. I was holding Sage in my arms and I arrived at the first dancer, a female elder, who touched Sage. I was hit by what felt like a jolt of electricity throughout my body. I began to sob immediately; I was not in control, I realized suddenly and completely, of anything. It was one of the most extraordinary experiences of my life.

This experience was repeated with each female dancer we passed. Each gave off a frequency or vibration that I had never felt before. I sobbed through the entire row. I received the same feeling from the men but, by that time at least knew what to expect, so managed at least a modicum of composure.

Sage was certainly blessed and her health was prayed for that day in the healing round.

I awoke well before sunrise the next morning, Sunday, in our hotel room at the tribal casino on the state's border with Nebraska. I drove by myself to the grounds in order to be there for the dancers as a supporter under the arbor. I knew it was the final day and that the men were preparing for their piercing round. It would be a difficult day for them.

I parked the truck just before the sun rose over the east end of the arbor and camp was fairly quiet. There was faint murmuring and stirring over on the west end, where the dancers had their camp under the arbor. I knew that they, as well as the drummers and singers, were waking and making preparations for the day.

There always seems to be much waiting in native ceremonies. If one is at all attached to schedules and deadlines, managing this requires a Jobian act of patience. Sundance is no exception. When I left the hotel before dawn, I was concerned that I was going to be late and miss the piercing round. It turned out that I probably sat for two hours before any dancing began and it was at least another four hours before the piercing round.

Everything that happened during my time at the dance came into laser focus during the piercing round. The energy and intensity just continued to build to fever pitch when the male dancers took their place under the tree. One by one, each had their chests pierced with eagle bones by Dino and his helper. The bones were then attached to their ropes, which had been hanging from the tree for the past four days, also patiently waiting for this moment.

At this point, all the male dancers were in the same position as the lone man I had seen at the tree on the first day. Each was now attached to the grandfather cottonwood tree with their ropes.

The female dancers were supporting around the circle, and the rest of the supporters were transfixed behind the dancers and under the arbor. Finally, the men were ready to offer their own small flesh sacrifice along with their prayers for the people. The tension was palpable.

After four approaches together to the tree, the men simultaneously ran backwards and pulled away from the tree. As they did, the ropes became taut and the bones were pulled from their chests. The ropes slackened, flew through the air, and came to repose on the ground between the dancers and the tree.

There was an immediate sense of relief and a celebratory mood as everyone knew that the dance had been successful; the prayers had gone out in all directions for all people and all things. There would be a closing round of dancing, the grandfather tree would be removed from the earth, the hole would be filled, and there would be food and fellowship.

LaRaye and Sage had arrived at the sundance grounds later that morning. During this last round of dancing, Sage's blood sugar had dropped and it was apparent to all of the dancers that she was there for healing. As my family was preparing to leave that Sunday afternoon in July 2012 to return to Chamberlain, each of the dancers, most of whom we had not met, approached us and offered to smoke their sacred pipes with us. They thanked us for the prayers and support that we had shared with them while they danced. They said it provided them with strength. It seemed as though we had known each other forever.

At some point, Dino approached me and asked me how I liked the sundance. I told him that it was one of the most powerful things I had ever witnessed. I thanked him on behalf of my family for the privilege of being there.

He surprised me and told me that I should be dancing with them in the circle. I laughed nervously and politely demurred. He pushed a little further though, and said he would provide me with a pipe if and when I changed my mind.

My new friend Clarence also teased me mercilessly that I should be out dancing. Although he joked with me, there was also some solemnity to what he said to me that made me take it seriously. He wanted me to not only dance, but also to ask a medicine man for healing for our daughter.

I vowed to consider all this before we left that day, but could not yet see myself as a part of that ceremony. I was overwhelmed by it, transformed by it and, in some way, found comfort and a home in it. But I resisted inserting myself into it. There is no question that my ethnicity held me back. A non-Indian taking part in a native ceremony was contentious.

Chapter 28

Medicine Wheel

Many traditional ceremonies, including inípi, crying for a vision, and sundance are considered by many Native Americans to be Native-only experiences. Many times, non-Natives are not allowed to participate. Sometimes, non-Natives are not even allowed to witness or be anywhere near the ceremony. I was definitely not going to upset that balance and truly didn't feel called to be in the center of the circle.

One of the things I love about Dino, after getting to know him more intimately over the course of many years, is his candor. He unapologetically told me, other dancers and anyone else who cared or had the ears to listen, that the sacred hoop has been broken for a long time. The colors of the wheel are black, red, yellow, and white and represent the connection between all of the different races here on mother earth.

The belief is that through human action – or inaction – we have ruptured the hoop and it is now broken. His sundancers are praying and dancing to bring it back together.

Dino's belief is that you cannot mend that hoop of all four colors when you exclude certain races or colors of people from praying and dancing together in the ceremony. He will be very clear with you that all races are needed to come together and that he can't tell someone whether they need to come to the dance to be a part of it or whether someone needs to leave the dance or should not be a part of it.

He says that is each individual's personal decision and is dictated by the spirits or the Creator, not by him or any other man, no matter their race or ethnicity. LaRayne and I wholeheartedly espouse this belief.

I may agree with Dino completely, but that didn't mean that I could necessarily envision MYSELF in what he and the other dancers were doing. It is one thing for me to believe in total inclusion and is quite another for me to presume that I should participate. LaRayne, on the other hand, could be a participant and I could see her continuing her Lakota spiritual path by being a part of it.

As we returned to another school year in the fall of 2012, Shawn and I continued to have conversations during "counseling sessions" about sundance, what I witnessed there and what everything meant.

Shawn shared a story with me about an inípi ceremony that had taken place during the four purification days that led up to the four days of dancing.

He had gone to get more wood to feed the fire, which keeps the stones scalding hot for the ceremony and must remain burning all through the days of preparation and then through the dance itself. Upon approaching one piece of wood, he saw that it was glowing and there was clearly the presence of a human-looking spirit or form in the wood.

Grandpa Dino told him to bring it into the lodge. During the inípi ceremony, Dino received a message that the wood was for healing medicine for the people. The spirits showed Dino where to collect the wood in that area and instructed him that the medicine would become available for Dino to give to the people if they asked for it and believed in it.

Naturally, this raised many questions for LaRayne and me. Shawn let us both know that the medicine was boiled in a certain way and then drank. I have always been intrigued by the idea that people had been treated successfully by spiritual men for as long as the Lakota people had been around.

I'd read books about the great Native leaders and medicine men such as Black Elk and Fools Crow. I knew that people came to them for healing and for other things that couldn't be explained by the rational or scientific mind.

Again, I believed these things had occurred, but simply couldn't imagine the possibility of them happening to me, or us. That said, a major stumbling block for my vision for healing Sage had been that LaRayne and I didn't know anybody well enough to be able to go into a ceremony with and to have them help Sage. Now, that block had largely been removed. I knew Shawn extremely well and was getting to know his grandfather Dino better.

I was dumbfounded that everything seemed to be falling into place for Sage that quickly. Thirteen years later, I understand completely that these things happen when they are supposed to happen and I don't have any doubt, only trust. LaRayne and I talked about asking for medicine for Sage. She was fully on board, so we committed.

Through Shawn, we asked Dino for medicine to heal our daughter's type 1 diabetes. Dino had also recently been diagnosed with type 1 diabetes and it had made his life extremely difficult. He agreed to give Sage medicine and suggested that I set up a lodge for inípi for the two of us. He would drive up on a Saturday morning, we would sweat together and he would share the medicine for Sage.

I was nervous and asked him what time of day was too early to sweat. He laughed at me and said you can sweat at any moment of the day. I found out later that he certainly had been going into ceremony at all hours of the day and night for years and years, and would be for years to come, often with me. Looking back now, my naïveté was staggering, but I couldn't know what I didn't know.

That Saturday morning, before the sun rose, I drove to St. Joe's campus. I covered the lodge and prepared the fire and the rocks for the inípi ceremony. Dino arrived that morning with his brother Dave, who had also been dancing for over 25 years at that point. We went into the lodge; Dino poured the water and led the ceremony.

After the first of four rounds, he asked Dave to move outside the lodge. When we were alone, he gifted me with the sacred pipe he had been dancing with for years and years. He instructed me that when it was my time to dance, I would know and that I would carry that pipe.

That pipe is one of the most important gifts I have ever been given. I was humbled that day. I did not deserve it, but it would be an egregious insult to refuse it. There are some who hold the opinion that non-Natives should not be allowed to carry a pipe and to pray with one for all people and all things in a good way. All I knew was that I had been given a most sacred gift and that there must be a reason which I could not then, nor maybe ever, fully understand.

I have the utmost respect for Dino and trusted what he was being told by the spirits to do. He instructed me to walk and to live in a good way with the pipe and to treat all people and things with respect. He told me there would be challenges that come with carrying the pipe, and I would have to face them. He told me that being a pipe holder is a hard road.

He also told me that I now needed to learn the songs in Lakota that came with the pipe and with the ceremonies. At that point in my life, I had been around the Native community every day for about 18 years. I had absorbed almost none of the language and certainly couldn't understand the songs.

My friend Schoeny could hear Lakota songs and almost immediately be able to sing them. It fits with his learning style. I, on the other hand, could hear the songs repeatedly and not be able to sing one of them. Nothing seemed to fit together and I couldn't recognize any patterns. I had the desire to learn, but apparently not the skill.

Even with a wife who taught Lakota culture and who was beginning to grow as a Lakota language teacher living in my house, I couldn't grasp it, and now I needed to. It was embarrassing.

A meal is always part of a traditional ceremony. Historically, generosity has been a core value or virtue of the Native American culture. Most possessions were not owned. They were community property and, as such, were shared. To give something to someone in need was not only respected, but also expected. Those who come to a ceremony are always fed. This is as important as the ceremony itself – no one should ever go hungry.

LaRayne takes this to heart and can seemingly provide a satisfying meal out of thin air, no matter the number of people or how much lead time she is given to prepare. When I first moved in with LaRayne and her girls, there was always a meal on the table and it was the hub of socialization in our house with conversation and laughter for as many as were at the table. I quickly gained 20 pounds and earned the nickname "chubby hubby" from the girls. It was a far cry from my bachelor life when I would stand in the kitchen over a microwaved burrito, plate optional.

Following the inípi at the school, where I was given the pipe, Dino, Dave and I came back to our house where

LaRayne had made a spread of soup, fry bread and chokecherry pudding for us. We visited with the two brothers and Dino left medicine with us to boil for Sage's healing. He said that when they had a ceremony in Rosebud later that fall, we would need to come down and Sage would receive healing at the doctoring ceremony. We were overjoyed and began our task.

In order to ask for help in a ceremony, it is common to offer tobacco to the leader as a traditional offering. We did this with Dino and went to the ceremony that November. It is not my place to share details of that ceremony, but I will say that Sage was given help and that LaRayne and I were asked by the spirits to commit to dance at the next year's sundance.

Chapter 29

Dave

At this point, our dancing in the circle was a no-brainer. Because of the gravity of what we were asking for our child, LaRayne and I agreed that refusal was not possible. We both committed to joining the dance circle of Helps the People sundance before we drove away from the tiny reservation town of Soldier Creek, South Dakota, where the ceremony was held that night.

Dino's brother Dave was hired to work with LaRayne in the Native American Studies department that fall. He and I became fast friends. He took me under his wing and began to teach me the songs. We began to hold inípi ceremonies together whenever we could – with the young men at St. Joe's, at the inípi at our house and in Soldier Creek, when we would travel down together for a monthly ceremony.

Dave lost the use of his legs in a car accident over 25 years before coming to work at St. Joe's. As a result, he was unable to help prepare the inípi ceremony, although I know he would have worked harder than anyone if he were able. I would prepare the fire and the rocks and the lodge, and then Dave would lead the ceremonies with the young men at St. Joe's.

It was a crash course, spending that much time with Dave and I learned much from him. LaRayne was also learning from him by working together in the classroom. He was an invaluable mentor as we prepared for next summer's sundance, which would be our first.

Dave Zephier is a very special person. He has almost no material possessions, is bound to a wheelchair and does not have the use of his legs. What he does have, though, is his sacred pipe, his spirituality and his understanding of the Native culture and ceremonies. As Dino had, Dave lived the ceremonies for the past 25 years and there wasn't much he hadn't seen.

He referred to LaRayne and me as babies because we were just learning, but he did it with patience and affection. It was a blessing to have a Native elder on campus who was able to lead ceremonies and to represent that ceremonial side of the culture to the kids.

At that point, LaRayne was yet unable to lead ceremonies and to pour water in the lodge. She and the school were still having difficulty finding women with the right to lead ceremony as an elder who also had the time to come to the school and perform the ceremony.

LaRayne and the girls were not able to have inípi ceremonies as often as the boys.

I will say that some spiritual leaders don't insist on males and females going into inípi separately. Dino does and he makes that very clear. Elmer passed this to Dino and Dino always said that it is too easy for men and women's minds to wander towards attraction and it could tarnish the ceremony.

I always liked the yin-yang balance of energy in a "mixed sweat," but I was now a part of Helps the People sundance and determined to follow the instruction. It simply wasn't my place to come in and begin to make those decisions for myself. This was not my world and I had no right – I can make my own decisions in my own world. LaRayne and I were in agreement and neither of us have been in a mixed inípi since we became part of that sundance.

As we prepared for sundance, Dave, LaRayne, Shawn and I had numerous conversations about the ceremony. We discussed the spirituality of it in general, and specifically referenced our Helps the People sundance. We talked about how difficult it was for most of the people who worked at our school or lived in our town to understand Dave's life experiences. This was especially true as he was living on the reservation and struggling day to day, But he was also living his traditional faith and having trust in the Great Spirit and the spirits at all times.

Most people here don't have any frame of knowledge or experience to be able to interact with him so, with a few exceptions, he was left alone while he was on our campus and in our town. On the other hand, Dave acknowledged that he had a difficult time fitting into our world, which was filled with administrative jargon and accreditation agencies that demanded we conform to necessary guidelines. Whether we like it or not, we live in a lawyers' world and organizations such as St. Joe's have to operate under numerous guidelines.

As a teacher, Dave was expected to draw up lesson plans and to interact with a campus with over 200 employees by e-mail, though he had little of that type of computer experience. He did not have a teaching degree or a technology degree, but what he had as a Lakota elder was invaluable. Unfortunately, our system demanded both. Just before the end of the year, St. Joe's and Dave parted ways.

It was a hard situation for both LaRayne and Dave, but neither of them can hold rancor for long and our relationship with Dave continued to grow over the seven years that we sundanced. He was at the center of the dance, singing and drumming while we danced, praying with us in the lodge and leading us all with his knowledge and his kind way of instructing ceremonial ways.

He was always present. That world was always comfortable for Dave. It was and is his home. Our world wasn't comfortable for him, although he did his best to attempt to conform to it while he was here, without losing who he was.

Chapter 30

Helps the People Sundance

LaRayne and I began dancing in July of 2013. We understood that we would be doing what was asked of us by the spirits in return for the good health that was given to Sage in her healing ceremony the previous fall. Some leaders believe in dancing one time, or one year, and being done. Some believe in a four or seven year commitment, which aligns with the two most sacred numbers for the Lakota people. Those numbers and patterns are intertwined with the natural world and the Lakota culture.

Dino, as taught by Elmer, believes that once you pick up the sacred pipe and begin to dance, the commitment remains for life. There are no magical numbers to dictate how long a spiritual life should endure, so it only makes sense that there is never an official time to retire, to hang up the pipe and quit dancing. When LaRayne and I danced that summer, we knew that we would do what was asked with all the reverence it deserved, until we were no longer able to do so.

Dino, and his dance, were no longer able to use the land halfway between Valentine, Nebraska and Mission,

South Dakota after 2012. So, for our first year, the dance was taking place in a new location on a hilltop just west of Soldier Creek community. There was ample room for the arbor and plenty of room for camping and parking all around the hilltop.

When we drove up the rutted, one-lane dirt and gravel road to the grounds in my truck for the first time, I immediately noticed that there were no trees near the proposed grounds, and therefore no shade. It was a blank slate of prairie grass, only touched by roaming cattle and prairie dogs, digging holes and tunnels wherever they pleased.

To the north, about a quarter mile away from where the arbor would be, the hilltop fell away and dropped gradually through trees and scrub-covered hills towards the actual Soldier Creek bottom, which was dry and lined with oak trees and thick underbrush. On a scouting trip for our own trees to cut for our arbor, we came upon a well-established dance arbor there. It was made out of sturdy store-bought fence posts, two by fours, and plywood. It was painted the colors of the four directions, black, red, yellow, and white. It was permanent and did not need to be rebuilt each year. Between the surrounding trees and the plywood cover, it provided natural and complete shade.

Dino prefers a more natural arbor, which requires a considerable amount of work each year to rebuild. A month after the dance, the pine boughs dry out and turn from a lush green to a light rust color. The needles become brittle and fall from the branches. They scatter on the ground and eventually mix with the winter snow and spring mud when those times come.

The oak crutches and stringers weather and weaken over time. They may crack and be unable to support the weight of the arbor as time goes. Many of the oak stringers are stolen. People become desperate for a source of heat in the winter and trespass onto the unoccupied sundance grounds, helping themselves to the bounty.

All of this necessitates a tremendous amount of work each year to prepare the arbor anew. I, too, love the idea of an all-natural arbor, although I often griped when I was out in the heat, performing back-breaking labor to make sure it was ready in time to provide some measure of shaded comfort for our supporters during the dance.

There were many times when I wished for a permanent arbor built by Lowe's and Menard's. Once it is complete, though, there is not a prettier sight than a well-done arbor, built through the cooperation of man and nature.

Although Soldier Creek likely did not flow very often, especially in July when we would be having Sundance, I was sometimes envious of the neighboring sundance next to the dry creek. It would certainly be nice to have the oak trees for shade – camping, a place to rest once the work was complete and for breaks during the day's labor.

At our dance on the hilltop with no trees, shade was always a luxury we couldn't afford. It usually needed to be the limited shade of an automobile or under tarps. Most camps for dancers and their families had blue plastic tarps attached in some fashion to oak posts that had been buried in the ground.

When the wind would blow, and it would always blow, the sound of all of the blue tarps flapping could be deafening.

Tarps were always in various states of disrepair, as the relentless wind would shred them in a matter of days. It became a toss-up: have a tarp to keep you out of the sun and occasional rain from a thunderstorm, or keep your sanity by not having to listen to the constant day-and-night slapping of the tarps.

LaRayne, Sage and I had an REI Kingdom Six tent with a rain fly and a gear garage. We also set up a nylon shade that we bought from the same sporting goods store. The gear was advertised for surviving events such as an assault on the summit of Everest, but had never been product tested through South Dakota summer wind or a thunderstorm at sundance in Soldier Creek.

Each year, our equipment would be bent diagonally to the ground or simply flattened. The tent would be shredded and would require patching and the poles would be twisted and mangled. I had to replace poles every year before finally finding a place somewhere in Washington that would actually fix the poles.

After experiencing this kind of windblown brutality on our temporary domiciles for several years, we ended up trying to make our own kitchen shelter out of oak posts. It worked better with canvas tarps and sturdy oak posts, but it still came with its own set of problems. We were always tinkering with the setup, tightening or slackening ropes and moving a shade canvas around to the side where the sun was shining through, depending on the time of day.

Most of the time, though, we were not in our camp. We were working. We were in the creek bottoms with no wind or on the hill tops with no shade, cutting, carrying, and lifting tree trunks or loading pine boughs, hundreds of them, on a flatbed trailer and then removing them and placing them on top of the arbor ten feet in the air. When we weren't cutting and lugging trees, we were digging post holes to make sure the oak trunks had a place to go after we drug them from the creek beds.

We also might be doing the same routine in order to build a cook shack for feeding the people who were coming to support the dancers. We might be in the creek bottoms, cutting willow to make sweat lodges, or repairing sweat lodge blankets and tarps, which had been destroyed by the wind.

Trips back to camp during the day were usually for a brief rest. They were needed in order to change a shirt that might be drenched with sweat and to get out of the sun, when possible, to guzzle as much water as a person could hold, and maybe to eat a little bit of food to keep the fuel up for the work to be accomplished. The last thing a person wanted to do when they returned to camp for respite was to have to fix the shelter or adjust the shade. There just wasn't any energy left for that. But it needed to be done, and no one was going to do it for you.

The manual labor was endless and necessary. Everything had to be ready to go by Wednesday when we brought the grandfather tree back to the grounds. There was always constant pressure to make sure things were done. There were also never enough people around to have many hands make light work. Dino's sundance is small. Each year that we danced, there were maybe seven or eight men and the same number of women dancing in the arbor. It was intimate.

We were able to really get to know the people we were dancing with. They became brothers and sisters. We were together 24/7, baring our souls in the sweat lodges, during work, and during the dance. Everything gets shared – all of life's problems, all the joys, mysteries and quirks. Everything. There was no shade from trees, and there was no shade to hide who we really were, our true selves. There was a high level of transparency between us, even at the baseline.

We quickly became an open book for each other and realized that we were part of this connected organism called sundance that needs to work in harmony in order to meet a common goal. The work done to prepare the grounds and to get things ready was just as important as the dancing and prayer. The same holds true for cooking meals and showing up to support. Everything is vital. This is one of the most important lessons I learned.

There is a concept of ikce wicasa in the Lakota language. It translates to "common man" or "simple man." It means that we are no one special. None of us. We are just simple people who are trying to humble ourselves in the face of everything there is.

I arrived at my first dance trying to do something specific for my daughter. I came to find out that literally everything I did was part of a bigger purpose. LaRayne and Sage and I all reaped rewards because of that understanding. We were all ikce wicasa and the universe has a way of letting us know when we are out of line.

Most are familiar with the saying "you get out of it what you put into it." The sundance is an intensely magnified example of that. For just over a week, you give absolutely everything you have, you sacrifice everything for everyone else and, in return, you are given amazing things that you never would have expected. I found out from "contributing for the common good" that I was not who I thought I was. It was a way of stripping the ego down to nothing.

Soon into our seven years of dancing, it became apparent that we were no longer just asking for help for our daughter and being asked to dance in return. We were getting ourselves and our egos out of the way to become a part of a tradition that relied completely on giving everything of ourselves to address a much larger and universal need.

During my first year of dancing, I still wasn't sure what to expect. I was told to make the preparations and show up and good things would happen, that I would know what to do. LaRayne sewed two skirts for me, to be worn over a pair of shorts. Both were red and blue with a circle in the middle of the front with a lightning bolt across it. It was my way of paying homage and respect to the thunder beings.

I used sage plants to make my wristlets and anklets and a crown for my head. I would link sage bundles and then tie them and wrap them in either red cloth or red felt and would wear them while dancing. Schoeny gifted me his eagle bone whistle, which would hang on the rope around my neck. At the end of the bone whistle was tied a small eagle plume.

He also gifted me two eagle wing spikes, the longest feathers on an eagle, to poke through my crown so they stuck straight up from it. My good friend Clarence White Horse, who had encouraged me to seek healing for Sage during my first trip to Dino's dance, gifted Sage with one eagle feather for each year that I danced. They were Sage's, but I was to carry them in the dance by tying them at the back of my crown and letting them hang.

That is generally what the men would wear, with some modifications in design to suit individuality. Women would wear dresses, usually hand sewn, that reached down to their ankles and covered their arms. Often, they would be in the colors of the medicine wheel or in green and blue to represent the sky or the earth. LaRayne sewed all of her dresses and even made some for the other women.

For a dancer, there is no playbook or manual with diagrams to tell you exactly where you are supposed to go once you are in the arbor. You are expected to know where you are going without necessarily being taught. Dino might not give you specific directions, but will certainly and clearly inform you afterwards if you did it wrong.

I sometimes referred to us, with pride, as the Bad News Bears of sundancing for quite a few reasons. One reason is that we never had enough money to buy what was necessary and we were always just piecing things together and scraping by. Another reason was that we were kind of a ragtag outfit.

Dino was sometimes incredibly patient with us. Other times, he would read us the riot act because we looked like the Keystone Cops, stumbling around in circles and bumping into each other. I like to think that was part of our charm.

It definitely brought laughter at times, too. Dino talked a lot about that balance. There was always an equilibrium that was there for happiness and sadness, for laughter and crying, for light and dark.

I often say "what the people need is a good laugh" and I mean it. The Native American culture is known for being very stoic, but the more you peel away the layers and get behind that facade, the more you realize that sense of humor is incredibly well developed and necessary for survival. I imagine that I either provoked levity and laughter on my first day or two, or I provoked frustration and anger from Dino, but I was trying my best. Again, I couldn't know what I didn't know.

Sometime during my first year, maybe on day two, we were coming out into the arbor for a round of dancing. It was midafternoon and I had a day plus under my belt; I was gaining confidence. While walking around the circle to my position, I noticed that my former student DJ, who was a supporter under the arbor, was pointing at me.

We usually don't pay attention to the supporters in that way because we are supposed to be focused on our prayer, but he was gesturing to me, so I gave him a thumbs up. I was proud because I assumed that he was pointing at how well I was dancing.

I proceeded down the line of dancers and my fellow dancer and true friend for life, Wopila Wesley was gesturing to me in the same manner. I nodded my head and smiled at him. It was pretty obvious that we both were in rhythm and sync and had our groove on. We were both blowing our whistles in time with the drum and the singers and it was one of those moments that just felt right, until Wesley broke formation and came over to tell me that I wasn't wearing a skirt. I looked down and saw that I had come out in nothing but my shorts.

The closest idea I can compare this to would be having the dream where I show up at my school in my underwear. However, when I wake up from that dream, everything shakes out just fine. I was never actually at my school in my skivvies.

This time at sundance, though, I was mildly embarrassed until I looked up from bare legs and realized that everyone had noticed. DJ and his family were having a good laugh at me. Wesley and the other dancers were either doubled over in laughter or, at the least, trying unsuccessfully to hide their laughter behind their hands.

I knew that Dino would not have a good laugh. He would not want me to leave formation and run into the rest area to put on my skirt and come back out into formation. Also, each move of individual dancers and the group around the medicine wheel was choreographed and had to be done a certain way. There was no way to go about my business unnoticed. I was screwed.

I knew I had no choice, though. I was going to be in a load of trouble if I just stood there and danced in a pair of shorts. I would probably be the only person in the history of sundancing to have ever done that. So, I spun in a circle, drawing even more of the already well-focused attention to myself, and walked or danced or ran, or whatever you want to call what I was doing, all the way around the circle of the arbor and exited to the rest area.

By now, there was no one there who was unaware of my predicament. I quickly pulled my skirt over my shorts and came back into the arbor. I did my spin and walked the correct path and found myself back in my place trying to act stoic about the whole thing. There were far too many people laughing about it.

It was a humbling moment and Dino did let me hear about it. But, in a way, I think it also ingratiated me to the others because they could see me as human and as someone who might make a mistake that all of us were capable of making. My buddy Wopila Wesley, once back in the rest area, laughed as hard as he could for as long as he could. Ever since that day he has called me, endearingly, Scotty No Skirt.

Eventually LaRayne and I wised up and stopped taking tents and shelters to the grounds to be torn up by the wind and storms. We began just taking two pickup trucks. One was my old beater with all of the tools, and the other was her newer one for us to sleep in and use as our home away from home. I would load up all of the tools that I had in my pickup along with all the rope I could buy from the hardware store because I knew that we would need all of it.

I can't count the number of times Dino asked me to do something that required skills or confidence I did not have. I wasn't raised to be a mechanic. I don't have much by way of auto mechanic skills and, even though I worked the summer of carpentry before graduate school, I was a grunt. I was following orders and didn't have the know-how.

Because of the small number of dancers and the small number of people who would actually show up pre-dance to help, I was forced into many learn-as-you-go situations. I had to figure out how to do something on the fly simply because no one else was there to do it and it wouldn't otherwise get done.

If Dino said to do it, I just did it, no questions asked. It needed to be done, whether I knew how to do it or not. I found myself in that situation many times over and I found my confidence growing as I did things I thought I couldn't do for the benefit of the sundance. As I said earlier, everything just seems to fall into place when and where it needs to if you keep showing up and keep trying to do the right thing with good intention.

Chapter 31

Spotted Eagle Boy

Through all of this, Shawn and I obliterated any kind of client/therapist therapeutic relationship boundaries that any of my colleagues and I had been taught in our clinical training. We were spending around 10 days together in the summer during sundance and we would often be at his grandpa Dino's house for monthly ceremonies on several Saturdays throughout the school year.

I came to know every member of his family and he became close with all of my family members. He was a sundance gadfly. He would wander around from camp to camp on the grounds, pulling up a chair (never his own), mooching food and drink, and freely visiting with all the people there. Everyone knew him and loved him – he had been doing this since he was old enough to understand how to go about socializing. He was welcome everywhere.

He would always spread sunshine and would ask about your family and how you were doing. He operated this way at school, too. He was well loved by the staff because he had that instinct to bond with everyone. Not many teenagers are confident enough to take the lead in building those kinds of relationships with adults. It could almost be a little alarming for the adults, but once they came to know Shawn, they understood that every part of his being was entirely sincere.

We continued to see each other in my office for weekly "counseling" sessions. I would see him around campus, I had him in my high school Sons of Tradition group, and he would go to inípi ceremony with me and the other high school students at St. Joe's. He led the drum group along with Schoeny and his uncle Dave, while Dave was working there. If there was something cultural happening, he was always going to find a way to be part of it.

Shawn was a big boy and loved to play football. He played for the Chamberlain high school football team and was proud to be an offensive and defensive lineman. He was able to move people around because of his size. He was one of the kindest people I knew, but wasn't afraid to mix it up on the field.

He worked hard and was going to earn a starting spot his senior year, but tore his ACL in the scrimmage leading up to the first game of the season. Losing his final season to play football was devastating for him, but he handled it well and never wavered from being the caring and gentle person he was.

When Shawn was in high school, a cultural issue arose. There was debate and then controversy about whether a traditional honor song could be played and sung by a drum group at the graduation for Chamberlain High School. Chamberlain always has a significant number of Native American students. St. Joe's usually has 40 to 50 students busing to the public school from our campus daily and there are many other native kids who come from the town of Chamberlain, as well as the neighboring reservation communities of Fort Thompson and Lower Brule.

Due to this large population of Native students, and because some stressed the importance of having an honor song as an expression of the culture, adults and students brought the issue of having an honor song at graduation before the school board. The proposed song would honor not only the Native students and graduates, but all the graduates from Chamberlain in any given year.

The school board had historically been unwilling to allow the song as part of the ceremony. Discussion, and sometimes arguments, ensued and the matter came to a head on December 9, 2013. The school board was scheduled to meet that night to discuss the issue as school board "for the last time," said then-president Rebecca Reimer. As if she and those board members would have the final say on when standing up against their discrimination could finally be put to rest.

The newspapers were present that night. A statewide television station sent a reporter and videographer to report on the event. The library at Chamberlain high school was filled to capacity with people, most of whom were in support of allowing an honor song at graduation.

I was there with LaRayne and Shawn. So were many of our St. Joe's students. They had come to support the idea of the honor song which, loosely translated, says "we follow the Lakota path, we are leaders, and we do this in a good way."

One of the imaginary obstacles the school board had often presented as a reason they could not include an honor song was that they were uncertain about the words. They wanted them written out before the song could be used. LaRayne wanted to help them understand the song, so she and I asked Shawn if he would be willing to sing the song for the school board after she explained the words.

In the Lakota way, as I've been taught, when you are asked to do something like this, you do not refuse. It is up to you to stand up and be a leader and do the right thing, no matter the challenges or consequences. Shawn was nervous, but agreed to do just that. He knew he needed to, but he also wanted to do it. With a good and sincere heart, he came to the meeting with us that night and we sat in the front row.

LaRayne introduced the song and made a plea to have it included at the graduation ceremony for all of our St. Joe's students and all of the Chamberlain students. She explained the words of the song and she asked, as is customary, for all in attendance to stand while Shawn sang the song in front of the school board, the audience, the newspaper reporters, and state wide television.

Shawn stood up and belted out a beautiful rendition of the honor song that would be sung at graduation. It took a tremendous amount of courage and, quite frankly, love on his part to do that. The Lakota nation was proud of Shawn that night. I know I was. I could only imagine the strength it must have taken for him to do that.

Two school board members, Dallas Thompson and Leanne Larsen, refused to stand. Everyone in the room, including most of the school board members, at least had the decency to honor this young man and his culture by standing for his song. Dallas Thompson went on record saying that he only stands for the American flag. I have yet to be able to forgive them for what they did to my friend Shawn that night.

The school board unanimously voted down the honor song again. It was disappointing and disheartening. Personally, I think graduation ceremonies are silly and I would be in full support if Sage was inclined to skip her own. But, if a group of people who make up a sizable segment of the school's population want to honor the graduates with a song to mark that rite of passage, I couldn't see the harm in that.

Sage was five and was getting ready to be a member of that school district. I was beginning to see the leaders of the district in a negative light that many of the decent and qualified teachers and administrators probably didn't want to be seen in. The meaningful and inclusive work they did with students daily was not being reflected by the decisions the school board was making.

To be a part of that situation in a positive way was representative of Shawn's character. He was not brash and he was not challenging. He would have reached across the aisle and shook the hand of anyone in that room that night, including the two who remained in their seats. It probably stung even more for that reason. Grown adults were intentionally disrespectful to him. They hurt him. On purpose.

Chapter 32

Blurred Vision

In the fall of 2013, several months after my first sundance, I caught a cold and sinus infection that was still raging after two months, which is very unusual. I had been extremely healthy for about eight years at that point, with no signs of Chronic Fatigue Syndrome. After two months, I finally had enough of feeling sick and visited the doctor. I was prescribed a couple rounds of antibiotics back to back, as well as a round of prednisone, just to clear all the pipes. None of it helped, so the doctor hit me with a very intense antibiotic called Levaquin.

On top of that, I had just been diagnosed with a cataract in my right eye by the local optometrist. I needed to travel to Sioux Falls for an appointment with the ophthalmologist, who would look at my eye and come up with a plan for the simple, routine surgery to give me a new lens. The day I went to Sioux Falls, I had taken my first dose of Levaquin, I was adjusting to a new prednisone dose and both eyes were dilated.

When I came home from Sioux Falls that night, I didn't sleep at all. Not one wink. I spent the entire night lying awake, paranoid. I thought I was losing my mind. I had been sick for a couple months and was tired of it, but that doesn't induce psychosis. Something was suddenly very wrong.

I made an appointment with my local doctor the next morning and reported what had happened after my first dose of Levaquin. I asked if withdrawal from prednisone could cause what I had experienced. He didn't think my reaction was normal, but humored me and took me off the Levaquin. A week or two later, I recovered from the sinus infection on my own and did not have a repeat of my wakeful night.

A month later, in January 2014, I had my cataract surgery. I felt great going in, but immediately after, didn't sleep. At least once a week, I was spending full nights awake in a panicked state of what felt, to me, like psychosis.

I struggled with this for the next six to eight months and desperately questioned what might be causing it. Overnight, I had been yanked back into the Chronic Fatigue days of old. It didn't make any sense. Nothing could have happened through the ophthalmologist and the surgery, or the dilation or the medication I was given that could – or should – have caused this relapse.

But there I was – back into the old pattern of several good days, then several bad days. I was miserable again like nothing had changed in the last eight years. It was as if it never left. Sage turned five and I turned into a sick, anxious, depressed father for the first time in her young life.

All the things I loved to do no longer interested me. All of the joy I found in being a father turned to sorrow. I could only see the beautiful things I was losing by not being able to connect with Sage due to my health.

I went to my niece's high school graduation in Brookings that May and spent most of it just hanging on for dear life, crying myself through the night in the motel room. It was bewildering and embarrassing. I put on a brave face in the best way I knew how, but inside I was crumbling.

I worried that, feeling this way, there was no chance I was going to be able to keep my commitment for sundance. It is too physically, mentally, and emotionally challenging to be part of that weeklong ceremony. I couldn't do it and, worse, I couldn't keep the commitment I had made to Sage, LaRayne, the other sundancers. Most importantly, I couldn't keep my commitment to the spirits who had asked me to dance.

I turned it over to Dino in the sweat lodge that spring and he helped me make sense of it by assuring me that there are two sides to everything. He told me to remember that, for all the good health and help that we receive, there is going to be some sickness and hardship that might come with it.

This was a test, he said. He urged me to be strong and to believe and to fight through it. He did not pity me. Dino knew suffering. He had done much of it himself while walking in that way and had witnessed it often with the people he loved.

I ended up sundancing in July that year and managed through the four days of preparation and purification and then the four days of dancing. It wasn't easy. I did it, though, and I was encouraged to pull myself out of whatever was happening to me by putting one foot in front of the other, one step at a time just like I did 20 years ago when illness first invaded my life.

A week or so after sundance, on a sultry Saturday morning in early August, I was riding a road bike across the river from Chamberlain, heading north on George Mickelson Road towards Cedar Shore Resort, where LaRayne used to work. There was a road construction site there. A thunderstorm hit the night before and the surface of the road was covered in run-off mud. The heat of the day was already oppressive and the top surface of the mud had become hard, dry clay.

As I steered my bike through the muddy construction zone, there was a car coming my way in the opposite lane and a car approaching behind me. There was no room for the three of us to occupy that same stretch of road, so I drifted to the right a little bit and went over the top of the dried clay. As I did, my bike tires discovered that it was greasy underneath from the wet of the night before. My back tire fishtailed. Before I could react, I was thrown to the ground on my back, which whiplashed the back of my head into the pavement.

The impact of my head on the pavement was the loudest sound I have ever heard. As I lay prone on the side of the road, I looked to my right and saw the river beyond the grass and trees on the bank. I didn't move initially and wondered if I had been unconscious momentarily. I didn't think so.

I sat up and took stock of the situation. My bike was quite a distance from me. My headphones had flown out of my ears, my water bottle was out in traffic, and there were still cars passing me in both directions on the road. I slowly rose to my feet and stood bent over on the shoulder, woozy from the violence of the impact. No one stopped to check on me.

I collected my things, inspected my bike for damage and made sure it would ride properly. I was very shaken and possibly concussed. I pedaled the two or three miles to our house and walked in the front door. I saw LaRayne and Sage cooking in the kitchen, told them that I had just had an accident, then I broke down and sobbed and sobbed.

My helmet had seven different cracks in it. Had I not been wearing it, I would certainly not be alive. I have been taking chances on bikes on dangerous trails in the mountains on rugged forest trails for the past 20 years. On this simple, slow, paved ride near my home on a Saturday morning, I had nearly lost my life because of a freak accident.

There was no question that I had my bell rung. We went to the Lower Brule powwow that same day to watch Sage dance and nothing felt right. Our school year began the next day and I went to greet the students and interact with parents and kids and staff on what was always a hectic day. In mid-afternoon, other staff noticed my state and told me I needed to go to the hospital and get checked out because I wasn't myself.

I went to the emergency room, was diagnosed with a concussion, and was instructed to miss work for the next week and then return to be re-assessed.

When things didn't improve after a week at home on the couch, I was told to stay in a dark room with no stimulation at all. No television, no phone, no lights. I was sick with Chronic Fatigue or whatever already and now was stuck in one place, in the dark, with a brain that wasn't functioning quite right.

Alarmingly, I was beginning to see numerous floaters of debris in my post-cataract right eye's visual field. I had nothing to do but lie in bed and watch them in a darkened room with no distractions all day and night. If I wasn't psychotic already, this would surely bring me to my breaking point.

Once the floaters became more than I thought seemed logical, I went to the optometrist to have him look at my eye. He dilated both eyes and told me that the right eye looked good, that the floaters were normal and that I would have to get used to them.

I called my optometrist friend from Minnesota, Garden Weasel, that night and explained the situation to him. He backed my optometrist. Later in the evening, I began to see shadows like a black curtains come across my right eye's visual field when I moved the eye.

I called the Weasel again and he told me to visit my optometrist again the next day. He commiserated that my optometrist would think I was crazy and second-guessing him.

He also told me to let him know if I saw flashing lights. I assured him that I didn't see flashing lights and he was relieved – that was a good sign.

That night, I went to bed scared to death of the concussion and the eye problems I was being told to just live with. When I turned out my light, I immediately began to see the dreaded flashes. I turned the light back on and called the Weasel to tell him I was seeing flashes of light now. He directed me to not wait and go see my optometrist first thing in the morning.

So, I showed up in the waiting room for my optometrist at 8:00 that morning after having closed the place down the prior evening at 5:00. He was surprised to see me and was possibly a little exasperated, but willing to humor me and have a look.

Once again, the eye was dilated. Almost immediately, he picked up the phone and called a retinal specialist from Sioux Falls. He informed him that my retina was in the process of tearing. The ophthalmologist was in Mitchell that day and they were able to secure an appointment for me later that morning.

LaRayne drove me to Mitchell, where the ophthalmologist dilated both of my eyes. He studied my bad eye and said that it was no longer detaching, which wasn't good news. It had actually detached since the first look in Chamberlain that morning. I needed to have surgery immediately the next morning in order to save the eye and my vision.

I walked out of his place and basically climbed up on my wife and had her carry me to the car as I fell apart. We sat in the car and I threw a leg over her and cried more as she tried to drive to the pharmacy to get me some of the recommended medications to prepare for the surgery the next morning.

Surgery was successful. Dr. Thomas repaired the tear and there were no complications. He performed a vitrectomy by taking all of the vitreous fluid out of it so he could cauterize the tear in the back of the eye on the retina. Then, he filled the eye with a giant gas bubble in order to keep pressure against the healing retina for the next month or two. The gas bubble would dissolve during that time and the eye would fill with its own supply of fluid during healing.

Post-operative instructions dictated that I lie on my left side so that the gas bubble would rise up and float against the upper right side of my right eye. I was to not move from that position for a week.

I suggested to the surgeon that what he was asking of me was not possible. I questioned how many people had actually lived through the recovery without a psychotic break. He assured me that everyone had and that I would be no different.

I didn't believe him.

Nonetheless, we returned home and I watched every single point of the 2014 U.S. Open tennis tournament through my left eye, which was squished into the couch. My right eye could see nothing because it had a gas bubble in it. The vision in that eye looked like, well, a gas bubble.

A week after surgery, I was given a green light to return to work and to stand and sit upright again. As the gas bubble slowly shrank, I would be able to see the tiniest edge of my vision.

The trick was that, as the bubble floated to the top of my eye, I should be able to see out of the bottom of my eye. In a hall of horrors optical illusion trick, though, the vision is flipped upside down. Even though the space the bubble left uncovered was on the bottom of my eye, what I saw was the very tip of the sky out of the top of my eye. It seemed enough to make a man finally, permanently, break.

Gradually, the sliver of sky grew into more sky and eventually the tops of trees and then more of the trees and then the tops of people's heads and then entire heads and then torsos. Finally, two months in, the gas bubble broke apart and multiplied through separation. Soon, the smaller break-off bubbles dissolved and I could see normally again.

I was thankful for the resolution of my visual difficulties, but I was left with lingering concussion symptoms and whatever Chronic Fatigue symptoms that had returned in January. The symptoms had certainly not been improved by the subsequent bike accident, concussion, retinal tear and surgery trauma.

My anxiety and depression continued to worsen and lasted through the end of the year and into 2015 before finally abating. I didn't know why it returned and I have no idea why it disappeared.

As before, once it was gone, I no longer concerned myself with it. Good riddance. My best guess from my studying and my experience is that it has something to do with immune system dysfunction and an experience in 2017 seems to bear that out.

Chapter 33

Nerves

Approaching the summer of 2017, I was experiencing tingling and numbness in my toes and continual spasms, or fasciculations, in my lower legs. The back of my calves looked like Sigourney Weaver's stomach when she gave birth to an alien back in the 1979 movie Alien. They writhed and wriggled uncontrollably and constantly.

I went to the doctor and assumed that the symptoms were probably harmless and I would be told to just live with them. I had never really been given any kind of legitimate diagnosis for many of the health problems I experienced in my life, so I figured she would just scratch her head and tell me that it was another mystery illness. Surprisingly, though, this local doctor was concerned enough that she sent me to Sioux Falls to meet with a neurologist who could perform an electromyography (EMG) on my extremities.

During an EMG, the neurologist pokes needles into your muscles and records the nerve responses when electrical currents are discharged into them. It is supposed to be slightly uncomfortable. In my case, the doctors were studying the nerves in my legs and arms to see just how far up any nerve problems might be occurring.

Every pulse was not slightly uncomfortable for me; it was excruciating. I don't know if I was uber-sensitive to the pain, but I was not handling it well. I was relieved when the test was complete and was given a tentative diagnosis of Chronic Inflammatory Demyelinating Polyneuropathy (CIDP).

She explained that this disorder is caused when the immune system attacks the peripheral nervous system. Whereas multiple sclerosis is more well-known and involves the immune system attacking the central nervous system, CIDP is the immune system over-responding and attacking the extremities.

She proposed it was a mild case, only affecting me sensorially, and not hampering any of my motor functions.

She suggested, as a result, I should take a watch-and-see approach. If it worsened, she said, the recommended first course of action would be for me to take long-term, high doses of prednisone.

I was still concerned that the prednisone I took back in December of 2013 (four years prior) had kickstarted my last round of chronic fatigue syndrome symptoms, so I felt like I was in a no-win situation. I could suffer as my mild symptoms worsened or ruin my body with prednisone and maybe have some relief from these symptoms.

There was only one more thing she needed to do to rule out other disorders and she could only do that with a spinal tap. In July 2017, I sundanced for my fifth year. I fasted from food and water for most of four days of dancing and was exhausted late on Sunday night when I returned home from Rosebud after 10 days there. I woke up early on Monday morning and drove to Sioux Falls for the spinal tap. It turned out to be a painless procedure for me.

Hospital staff called me the day after the tap and then two days later at noon to ask how I was holding up. I told them I was fine and was thinking about going to work out that afternoon. They advised me to wait another day before doing anything strenuous and told me they would check in with me on the third day.

I hung up the phone and was immediately clobbered by a headache of an intensity and nature that I had never experienced before. It forced me to the ground. If I sat upright, I was struck with excruciating pain, couldn't make sense of anything happening around me, and I couldn't carry on a conversation.

I immediately contacted the hospital in Sioux Falls and informed them things had gone south. I explained the symptoms and they confirmed that I was having a spinal headache. They told me that the injection site in my lower spine from Monday's tap had not properly sealed itself. It was dripping minute amounts of cerebrospinal fluid (CSF), resulting in an ever-so-slight imbalance in the volume of CSF in my central nervous system.

The volume changed rapidly upon standing or sitting up, which caused the excruciating headaches and disequilibrium. The only relief would be to stay in a prone position until they could get me back to the hospital for the fix, which would not be until two days later.

Two days later, LaRayne again drove me to Sioux Falls. I laid on the bench outside the hospital for a while and then laid on my side in the waiting room and then laid down in the hospital room until they could come in and take blood from me. They put it back into the initial injection site on my spine so that it would form a clot over the small hole and would no longer leak. It is a miracle cure. A couple of days later, I felt back to normal.

My CIDP symptoms seemed to have worsened, though. The spinal tap had ruled out other problems, so I reluctantly agreed to begin taking prednisone to quell the symptoms before they grew too severe.

A couple of months into taking the mega doses, though, I began to reflect on Sage's healing ceremony and about our own experiences through sundance. I made the decision to offer my pipe filled with tobacco to Dino to ask him for healing for my condition.

He agreed and in November 2017 I had my own healing ceremony down in Rosebud. I won't share details of that ceremony out of respect. It is not my place to do so.

I was also given my Lakota name that night. Dino wanted all of the dancers to have a Lakota name so that the spirits would recognize us in ceremony and would know who we were when we made our final journey to the spirit world.

The spirits gave him a vision that night during my healing ceremony and from that my Lakota name was given. It is Inyan Ska Oyate Obmani, or One Who Walks With the White Stone Nation. I humbly accepted that gift and vowed to try every day to understand it and to honor it.

Through it all, I tried my best to follow my friend Dino's path set forth for his sundance by the spirits. It is not my place to tell him what is right and what is wrong, and I trust him completely when it comes to the traditional ways. I love him and he is a good friend.

In the end, though, I let him down, I'm afraid.

Our seventh year of dancing was in 2019. By that point I had seen many people come and go from the dance. I watched some abuse Dino's notions of how sundance should be conducted.

I saw others who disregarded his expectations for the tradition. He and I often lamented these transgressions together. He considered me one of his leaders and I was a right hand man to him. He depended on me.

A couple of people had left after the dance in 2019. They had bad experiences and blamed the dance for their troubles. I didn't feel the same. I felt that the dance had been the best of all of my seven and that my family and I had been blessed beyond anything I had ever dreamed.

I didn't deserve any of it, but there it was. By participating in the dance, by completing the work, and simply by being a part of Helps the People sundance, I was receiving good things. I was floating on air and was prepared to dance forever. My belief in the traditional ways was stronger than ever.

Chapter 34

Shawn's Journey

After graduating from Chamberlain high school with no honor song at the ceremony in 2014, Shawn had enrolled in the welding program at Mitchell Technical Institute.

He had quite a bit of special help in high school and found himself unable to find his footing in bigger classes with teachers who didn't know him in Mitchell. He dropped out after a semester and moved back to Valentine to be near his grandpa, mother, and many family members.

He had a girlfriend and they lived together. They worked and were always part of ceremonies. Around 2019, his girlfriend took a job in Chamberlain as a nurse and Shawn became a houseparent at St. Joe's. He was going to fulfill a dream to give back what was given to him when he was a student.

That year, 2019, Shawn also finally pledged to dance the next year in the sundance. He had a pipe and it had always been a simple matter of time before this would happen. It was preordained. He was aware that it was going to happen someday, but was also rightfully scared of it.

He and grandpa Dino didn't want him to do it until he was ready and Dino did not push him. His family members often teased him about not being ready, about being a big baby, and not being able to do it, but they all knew that he was going to do it eventually.

In fact, all of us knew that he would one day be the leader of the sundance once grandpa was gone. Shawn had been the one to whom the medicine presented itself, after all. It was shown to him in the wood pile at the sundance several years prior, not to grandpa Dino.

Grandpa knew that Shawn was the future and that the sundance altar would go to him or he would be given his own by the spirits. That story remained to be written.

When Shawn pledged to dance in 2019, I was with the rest of the sundancers in the center of the circle on the last day. After the piercing round there were cheers and tears and smiles all around when Shawn pledged. We had all watched Shawn grow up around sundance; we all loved him and were rooting for him.

It brought a special happiness to all of us. It brought a special happiness to me because he was my student and because he felt like a son to me from our experiences at St. Joe's and then through the sundance.

He came to work at St. Joe's that fall and immediately fell in love with the job and the kids. In return, they immediately fell in love with him. He understood them and their experiences and they understood him. He knew intimately where they had come from and the experiences they went through when they were at St. Joe's.

He brought his cultural knowledge to the drum group and other cultural happenings at the school. He was invaluable to our overall culture, Lakota and otherwise, and he was excited to be at the school.

In January 2020, a simple man-made scheduling conflict interfered with me being able to attend the sundance later that summer. We had scheduled 2020's dance a year ahead of time at the end of the 2019 dance. I made a plan with my Woster extended family specifically to accommodate the 2020 scheduled sundance date.

In January 2020, Dino and other sundance members changed the date set for the dance that summer. I asked Dino to keep the sundance date where it had been scheduled since the previous sundance, but he ultimately moved it to the weekend when he knew that I would be unavailable.

In doing so, he forced me to make a decision and to face a test. Ultimately, I had to break my commitment to the dance that summer and knew I couldn't go halfway. I was either full-on or full-off. My commitment from the beginning had been complete and breaking even part of my commitment, to me, was just like breaking it completely and forever.

It was one of the most difficult decisions I have ever made, but, once I made it, I knew I needed to stand by it. I had my own mind.

I didn't break my commitment to the altar, to the pipe, to Dino, to the other dancers, or to the spirits, but I did break my commitment to a man-made calendar and couldn't see any other way. COVID arrived shortly after that in March 2020 and I thought maybe the dance would be called off, but they carried it out and Shawn was able to dance for the first time, but without me in the circle.

We were both disappointed that we were not able to dance together. We were both counting on it. Either way, he was fine. He always had inside him what he needed in order to be strong in the arbor. And, of course, he had his own mind.

Shawn was incapable of holding a grudge and there was nothing that could hurt our relationship. We were too close for that. So, when he returned for the school year of 2020- 2021 the fall after his first sundance, we worked well together as a team with the boys in his homes at the school. It was one of the best years I have had at St. Joe's and a large part of it was due to being able to work with Shawn in such an intimate, intense capacity.

In the summer of 2021, Shawn had just proposed to his sweetheart of several years and he couldn't have been more excited. He showed many people in his family and at the school the engagement ring and told them the story of how he had asked her to marry him.

He loved her and wanted to have children with her when the time was right. He looked forward to his second year of sundancing, which would be happening in July. Life was wonderful for him and his fiancé.

Around the Fourth of July that year, Shawn became very ill. When it became bad enough, he was taken to the hospital in Chamberlain. He tested positive for COVID.

He would suffer some, we all collectively figured, but would get the treatment he needed at the hospital and would be released. Later that month, his cup would be filled at sundance. That would be the end of that story. He would be back on the path again. The red road.

But Shawn was obese, maybe morbidly, and his health wasn't great to begin with. He did not make the quick recovery we all – Shawn included – hoped for and expected. He had more severe trouble with his lungs and chest and was taken to a larger hospital in Sioux Falls to receive more intense care.

Because of the highly contagious nature of COVID, Shawn was not allowed any visitors in the hospital, not even his fiancé. I talked to him on the phone several times while he was in the hospital and he was always in good spirits. He missed contact with family and friends, but was managing and knew it was only a matter of time.

Of course, he only wanted to know how we were doing. He admitted that he didn't feel good, but was getting better and knew that things were going to continue to improve.

Unfortunately, he wasn't better when the purification days for sundance arrived and he was unable to go. He remained in the hospital in Sioux Falls and knew that the entire sundance would be sending prayers his way during the full week of ceremony. That would make everything better.

I spoke with him on the Friday of sundance week, which is the second day of dancing. We talked that night and he said he had been in contact with many people who were in and around sundance. He was thankful and strengthened by the fact that they were sending prayers. He was finally able to see his fiancé and the visit had lifted his spirits.

He said he was much better and was expecting to get out over the weekend and thought he could possibly make it there for the last day of sundance. However, the medical staff wasn't willing to release him and he was still there during piercing day on Sunday. He was there on Monday, the day after the dance, still expecting to be released soon and to make a full recovery.

Sometime on Monday, though, things worsened for Shawn. His grandpa Dino, his fiancé, and his mother drove to Sioux Falls to be with him. He told them that he didn't feel well and was scared. He had acute difficulty breathing and eventually slipped into unconsciousness.

The medical staff worked on him and eventually his grandpa Dino had to make the difficult decision to let him go.

Shawn was the love of Dino's life. All of their plans for their future together were wiped away and Dino was left with a gaping hole in his heart. The plans for Shawn as the future leader of the sundance slipped away that day, too.

LaRayne and I were a part of Shawn's funeral ceremonies over the course of a few days. Fittingly, Dino had a traditional funeral at the sundance grounds. The funeral home brought Shawn's casket in their hearse. We had a caravan of cars and crossed the reservation to the hilltop above Soldier Creek, where sundance had ended the previous weekend.

The lead seven vehicles each had a flag tied to them that had the colors of the main seven colors of our sundance. Our truck had a yellow flag for the east and it remained attached to our mirror for the better part of a year until it disintegrated from the wind and weather.

Once we arrived at the grounds, horses led Shawn's casket up the last of the gravel road on the approach to the grounds. We carried it into a tipi which had generators powering air conditioners to keep the inside of the tipi somewhat cool on those scorching early August days and nights in order to preserve his body through the wake.

I stood in front of the tipi and was able to eulogize Shawn and talk about my vision of what he meant to all of us. Dino did the same.

Dino had inípi ceremonies for men and women. We prayed, we ate, we told stories about Shawn, we laughed and cried over him, and we missed him. He always brought us together. He was the common thread for so many of us.

I wouldn't have been near a ceremony and wouldn't have asked for healing for Sage or myself if it hadn't been for Shawn entering my life as a seventh grader.

I watched him at sundance and at ceremony. He was good to everyone and everyone loved him. Even in death, he brought us all together for his weekend funeral ceremonies. He was our connection.

For Shawn's final dance, his fellow sundancers, former housemates and staff from St. Joe's, friends, and family carried his casket into the center of the sundance grounds where the grandfather tree would normally be and, with Dino directing us, we danced to the directions in communion with the spirits.

As always, we were accompanied by the heartbeat of the drum, the shrill whistles of the eagle bones, and the cries of the singers.

When it was time, Dino let us loose and we danced with abandon all over the circle in celebration of the life of this remarkable young sundancer who was loved by all of us.

Epilogue

I reflect on Shawn now and I don't suffer sadness or pain. I didn't even feel much heartache in the beginning, except for a profound sense of loss – for those kids who won't have the blessing of having him work with them at the school, for his family who won't be able to share his love, and for his fiancé who wouldn't be able to realize their shared dream of a life together with children to raise.

I trust that Shawn is just as much a part of me and my world as he ever was. The spirit of Wanbli Gleska Hoksila, Shawn's Lakota name for meeting the spirits, is with me at all times.

When I go into the sweat lodge with a group of boys from the school, he is always there. His singing was always earthshaking and was the biggest presence in the half dome of the lodge. You couldn't miss it. I can't hear him singing anymore, but his silence is deafening. That's how big his presence was, and still is.

Shawn gifted me a star quilt when he graduated from high school. It hangs prominently on the north wall of my office. Next to it is a star quilt I received from his cousin Kenyon, another of my younger students. Kenyon lived in Shawn's home at our school and also lived with Shawn in Chamberlain during the summer so he could attend local basketball camps with Chamberlain's team.

At Shawn's funeral, the funeral home workers did not remain at the grounds. I assume they did not want to be liable for having a body out in that heat. They left Shawn's body with us and I acted as a sort of de facto funeral director for those two days, guiding people into the tipi for viewing.

Before we carried him into the center of the arbor for his last dance, we completed visitation and viewing and closed the casket for the final time. Dino asked me to close the casket. The last person in the tipi with me was Kenyon. Together, we covered Shawn in the lace and pillowed silk of the inside curtains of the casket and then we closed the lid together. Forever.

The Zephier family gave me a star quilt for St. Joe's at the funeral. It hangs in the hallway outside of my office on the counseling floor at the school. When Shawn's boys and I walk past it, we put our palm on it and run our hand across it. We do this in remembrance of him; he is gone at St. Joe's, but he is not even close to being forgotten. He is always with us.

As I remember Shawn, I reflect on the time I lay face down in the hard packed dirt on a hill near Soldier Creek, in the meager shade under the arbor during a rest break from a round of dancing.

I had been in the middle of giving flesh offerings, tiny bits of skin carved from my shoulder by another dancer with a needle and razor, which were to be tied up in a red cloth, strung together with the offerings of others, and tied to the tree as an offering for people who were suffering.

I had never had difficulty with giving flesh or with the piercing round. Something had gone wrong this time, though, and I sank to my knees. I struggled to remain conscious. My vision came and went. I alternated between seeing black and then the grandfather tree, rooted firmly in the center, wrapped in the prayer ties and flags the dancers had tied in preparation for the dance.

There were hundreds of cloth squares filled with tobacco, tied, and strung together and wrapped around the tree. Each tobacco tie was filled with prayers and hope for the people who were and are suffering in this world. Some held specific prayers, some were for healing for every living thing.

Tobacco-filled cloth flags, each a yard long, hung from the branches. They fluttered and swayed in the unceasing prairie breeze. They were black for the west, red for the north, yellow for the east, white for the south, blue for the sky, green for the earth, and purple for the thunder beings. They, too, held the prayers and hope for the people from the sundancers.

Lying there, I was surrounded by prayer. My prayers, the prayers of the other sundancers, the prayers of everyone who comes together to offer them in a good way, with a good heart, for those suffering in this world.

The prayers rose from the ground, fell from the sky, were carried by the four-leggeds, were walked by the two-leggeds, and were washed in by the swimmers.

The trees and the plants the prayers grew from were everywhere and reflected the connections we all have to each other.

As I lay there, on my knees, I held the sundance pipe and did not let go. I thought about, prayed about, and came to understand the arc of my life.

My red road was filled with mistakes, learning, understanding, forgiveness, grace, and love. The blessings were innumerable and immeasurable.
My hope and belief were overflowing.

Hetchetu alo (that is all I have to say).
Mitakuye oyasin (we are all related).

Dad and me playing guitar when I was three in 1972.

The Woster cousins gathered around Grandma Marie as she played piano when I was five or six.

Scares the Pie, Pitbull, Brad Aames and Garden Weasel at the Pierre mall in yet another lip-sync show in 1985.

GOVE

RIGGS HIGH GOVERNOR PIERRE, SD 57501

Ries, Woster el

GIVING SPEECHES . . . New Mayor and Vice Mayor Ries and Woster. (Photo b

Garden Weasel and me stumping for mayor and vice mayor of Pierre TF Riggs high school in 1986.

My 1987 senior picture complete with flannel and bandana around my neck.

My first home in Fargo where my parents took a picture as they drove away and left me alone there in the fall of 1991.

The crowd scene from Soldier Field, where I am part of the psychedelic multitude in 1992.

My sister and me at her wedding in 1992.

My mom and me in front of Orange Sunshine the day I left for Austin, Texas in January 1994.

Schoeny, LaRayne and me at the local triathlon in 2004.

LaRayne at our wedding spot on Nancy's beach on our Ides of March engagement day in 2006.

Smudging my great grandmother's ring following my proposal and LaRayne's acceptance. I am wearing the ring that LaRayne picked up for me at Ferley's Jewelry Store in Pierre that day.

My great grandparents Ada and John Leiferman with the ring on their wedding day in 1906.

LaRayne at the one-year memorial giveaway in 2006 to honor Trevis' life.

The Henry and Marie Woster farm wedding with my relative Ron "Red" McManus, beloved mayor of Reliance, officiating in 2006. Legend has it that we are the only couple that he ever married that is still together.

The wedding spot on Lake Oahe with officiant Mark Schoenhard the day after the farm wedding.

Giving a star quilt to my parents on our wedding day.

Hiking to the top of Bear Butte with Sage when she was one and a half in 2009.

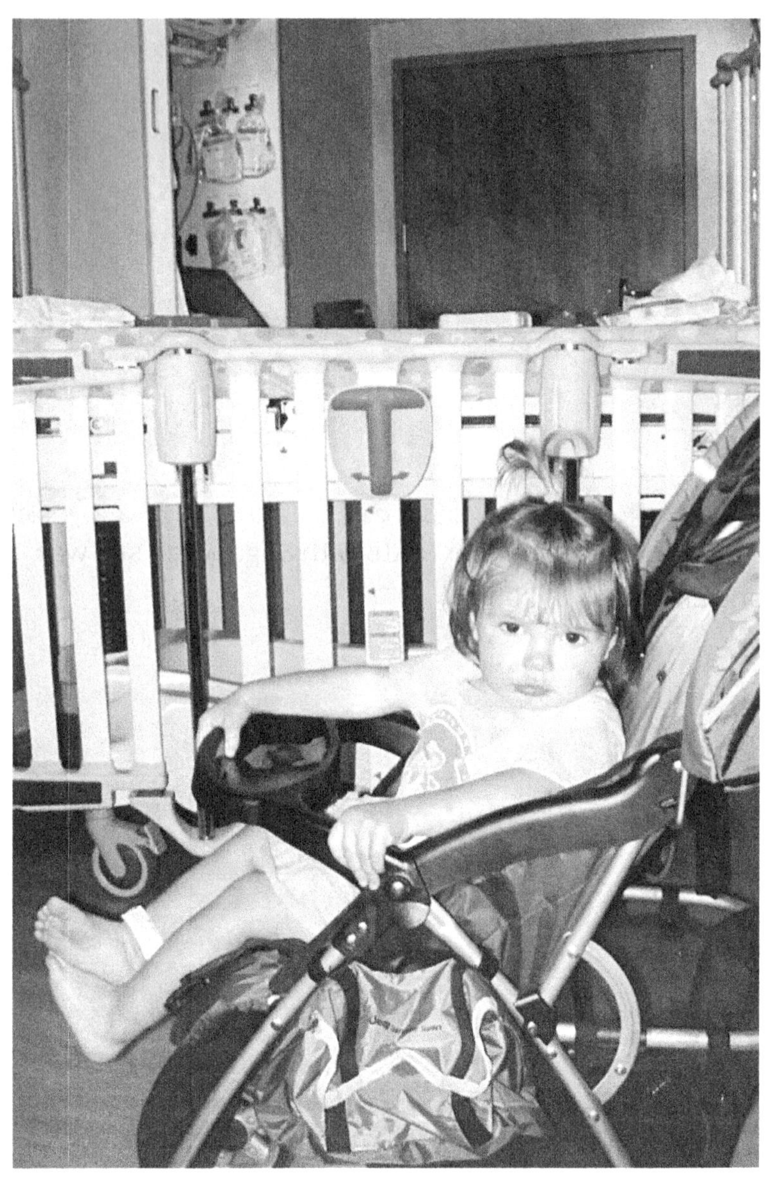

Sage looking pissed a week after her diabetes diagnosis at Sanford Children's Castle in July 2009.

Sage in her pink jingle dress outfit at the Lower Brule powwow in 2013.

Sage as Little Miss Chamberlain High School with Miss Indian World at the Lower Brule powwow in 2014.

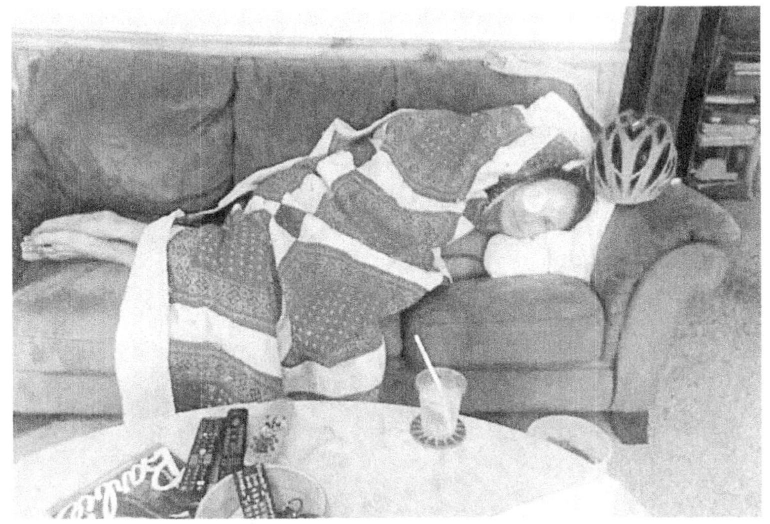

Me after my retinal repair surgery in August 2014.

Shawn during his high school football years.

Shawn helping with our family sweat lodge in late summer 2019.

Jackie, Jordan, LaRayne, Frankie and Sage at St. Joseph's powwow in 2025.

LaRayne and me with our grandkids at St. Joseph's powwow in 2025.

Acknowledgements

I'd like to acknowledge all the people who made this book and life possible beginning with my first guides, mom and dad, Nancy and Terry Woster. There simply aren't better parents. You did everything right.

Shawn, Dino and Dave Zephier have been my friends and mentors along the Lakota spiritual and ceremonial pathway.

John Beheler has been as well. Thank you for your friendship and for sharing your own story, koda. Thanks for the stunning cover artwork. What a gift!

Chronic Fatigue Syndrome – I hate your guts, but I learned so much from you.

LaRayne Woster showed me how to give until you can't give anymore, and then showed me how it all gives back so there is even more to give. Plus, you likely rescued me from Chronic Fatigue Syndrome. I love you.

Jackie, Jordan, and Frankie accepted me into their lives when it was probably the last thing they wanted to do. Thanks for allowing me to be part of your family.

Sage, Jordan, and Frankie (and now Cedar) taught me how horrible Type 1 diabetes is but, more importantly, how to persevere and thrive day-to-day while living with a life-threatening disease. I'm amazed by your strength.

My old pal Schoeny introduced me to new ideas daily and continues to challenge my comfort zone.

All my students and their families over the past 31 years have taught me about friendship, trust, and loyalty. Thanks for being part of my family and allowing me to be part of yours.

To my favorite authors, musicians, artists and gurus – I heard what you were putting out there. I'm glad I was paying attention.

I'm a shade different and, hopefully, a shade better person each new morning. At the least, I'm striving because of all of you.

About the Author

Scott, a committed counselor at St. Joseph's Indian School since 1994, employs his deep understanding of Native American education to enlighten and inspire. As the host of the school's podcast, Hochoka (center of the camp circle), he continues to discuss issues critical to Native American education.

Scott's life isn't just about work. With his wife LaRayne, he has raised four daughters and revels in the joy of seven grandchildren. Outside of work and family, he unleashes his creative side by writing songs and performing them on guitar in his one-man band, The Ways and Means. He has a love for the natural world and can often be found with his mountain bike and his camper van, Thelma the Moveable Feast, somewhere in the mountains or deserts of North America. Scott's multi-faceted life experiences seep into his writing, creating a tapestry of vivid storytelling that resonates with readers.

Made in the USA
Coppell, TX
24 February 2026

72241937R00207